Praise for *At*  *1*

"Reminiscent of Sandra Cisnero's *The House on Mango Street* with its lyrical voice and tender narrator, *At the Narrow Waist of the World* is a gorgeously vivid memoir that blends the Spanish of the author's native home and the English of her adopted country to describe the weight of events and a larger-than-life mother who confounds family and psychiatrists alike. The book pulses like a constellation in the night sky."

—Jimin Han, author of *A Small Revolution*

"In this lyrical chronicle about a girl growing up Jewish in Panama, we learn from Marlena Baraf that it is possible to live on that narrow edge between countries, languages, and spiritual homes."

—Ruth Behar, author of *Lucky Broken Girl* and
An Island Called Home: Returning to Jewish Cuba

"Marlena Maduro Baraf's compelling memoir, *At the Narrow Waist of the World*, transports us into her Panamanian childhood in the 1950s and 1960s, when her enchanting mother succumbs to mental illness and is sent away for years at a time. Baraf's writing is lush, immersing us in the scent of hot days and bougainvillea, the sounds of children's games and family feasts, and the colorful, beautiful dresses of her mother and aunts. The book's dance between Spanish and English fills it with a musical beauty, revealing the love and support of this remarkable family."

—Elizabeth Garber, author of *Implosion:
A Memoir of an Architect's Daughter*

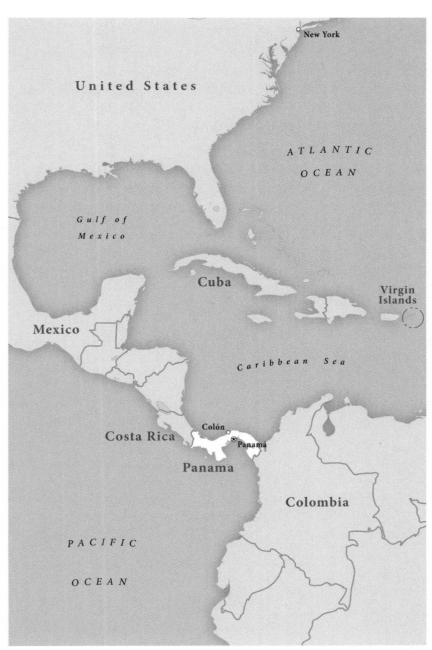

map by Mike Morgenfeld

AT the NARROW
WAIST of the WORLD

AT the NARROW
WAIST of the WORLD

a memoir

Marlena Maduro Baraf

SHE WRITES PRESS

Published August 2019
Printed in the United States of America
Print ISBN: 978-1-63152-588-9
E-ISBN: 978-1-63152-589-6
Library of Congress Control Number: 2019935694

For information, address:
She Writes Press
1569 Solano Ave #546
Berkeley, CA 94707

She Writes Press is a division of SparkPoint Studio, LLC.

The author is grateful to the following literary journals where parts of this memoir were first published as essays. "Mami" was published in The Westchester Review; "La Misa," in Blue Lyra Review; "Days of Opera," in Lumina; "Sweet Tarts," in Streetlight Magazine.

This story is true as it happened to me. But it also belongs to other individuals in my family and to the collective "family" that in Latin America embraces a much larger group. We are tightly woven in the cloth. Others' recollections and tender memories will be different from mine. This is the nature of life. Here is my truth at this moment in time.

Most names have remained the same. A few have been changed to preserve the privacy of certain individuals.

Para Patricia, Carlos, y Roberto

CONTENTS

A NOTE TO READERS

When I began to write this story, I found that it became impossible to strip it of my language of birth. Spanish expressions came loaded with meanings dragging behind—cans tied to the back of cars of newly wed couples, strings of story and culture. The tale would be untrue. Clearly at a colossal distance from experiences that took place in a Spanish-speaking world.

Tone of voice, a phrase, a snapshot in my mind—this is how my memories began, fragments remembered and raw feelings leading me to a predestined accounting. My mother—*mami*—had an undiagnosed mental illness. She was taken to psychiatric hospitals when I was a girl and young woman. Here is the story of loving her—and holding her at a distance, a self-protective reflex that set me on a Panama–United States journey and changed the center of my world.

Llegó el aguacero, the calls announcing the arrival of pounding rain, are roped to the image of maids in white, *horquillas*—clothespins—between their teeth, fingers pulling towels from clotheslines, my excitement at the rumbling cascade of thunder.

My mother said, "*Me quieren matar,*" the maids want to kill me. That scoundrel, poison! She said *matar,* accent on the second syllable, more fluid and prolonged than "kill," which can happen with a single bullet. *"Están gordas,"* she told us. Not, "You are fat." *Gordas* is fuller, richer in meaning, linked to Colombian artist Botero's corpulent figures more than to the derisive and simplified, "fat." And a *teta* is not a breast, not even a tit.

"Judía," with the harsh *jota* sound, meaning "Jew," arrived chained to ancient epithets, loathing, and fears, though my Sephardic Jewish family was generally treated with delicacy in a country of easygoing people who lived in a steaming heat that was almost impossible to escape.

Expressions that individuals in my family used brought the person and issues to life. *"¿Con quién andas?"* "Whom do you walk with? "Who are your friends?" is linked evermore with my grandmother, Amamá, who worried that we wouldn't be accepted in Catholic society. *"¿Qué me está pasando?"* was a recurring refrain from mami as she poked at her throat, or her chest, or her lungs. "What is happening to me?"

Toys that I went to *tío* Felix's store to select are not the same as the *juguetes* we played with. The extra syllables in the Spanish word "juguetes" extend the pleasure of my *patines* and *muñecas.* "I'll pay you back, *te lo prometo,"* my brother Carlitos said, *"te lo prometo."* The English, "I promise," does not ring as true. In Spanish, Carlitos used the intimate, "I promise it to you."

The words chose me, the ones that expressed a fuller meaning or played a better tune with English, the flexible language of my more recent acquaintance. I have provided translations in most cases so that non-Spanish speakers are not left behind, but I've left some Spanish expressions untouched, as they are part of the fabric of my youth.

CENTRO DEL MUNDO

Concolón

In the 1950s the country of Panama was small—about 750,000 people. We lived in the capital city and knew everyone who was white and the people surrounding our lives who were darker, un *café-con-leche* mix *típico de Panama*. Indian and white—*mestizo*. *Blancos* like me were usually of European descent. Native *indios* lived in clusters in remote parts of the nation. *Negros*, many who were descendants of laborers who had built the canal, lived mostly on the Caribbean side. We had *chinos* whose ancestors came to build the railroad, merchants from Greece, India, Italy, and Spain, and the *Americanos* who lived in the Canal Zone. *Panameños* called this *"un concolón,"* like the rice at the bottom of the pot, golden and white and black and brown.

Patricia

Anita, who was seven like me, lived next door, and she had thick, black hair that her mother brushed every morning fifty times before weaving it into two lustrous braids to the middle of Anita's back. My sister Patricia couldn't resist, and I watched, secretly thrilled, standing at the far side of the small garage, when Anita, *ojos como pepas,* felt the clunky scissors slicing across her tresses. It ended with Anita in tears and one dead braid on the ground. Patricia remained in the garage for hours, crouched behind the bumper of an old Chrysler. I ran indoors and crawled under the bed.

"¡Llegó el aguacero!" the maids called out. There were several voices calling, echoes from the houses along the street. *"¡Llegó el aguacero!"* was shorthand for "run outside and pull the clothes from the line before they get soaked." When I heard the lilting cries, I knew to get out of my clothes down to my panties and go outside to play. I was saved, but Patricia was not. Tía Mimí—one of *papi's* sisters—was living with us then instead of mami, and she was worried about the trouble. Patricia had to visit Anita's mother that night with papi. I had to hold my guilt inside, and that was worse.

Patricia cut the sleeves off her dresses, or the neckline, or hem. She made capes and skirts for her dolls. When she was wielding the scissors and working the needle and thread, nothing else existed. I played with dolls in the customary way, making up stories, while Patricia fashioned wardrobes for her little models.

When we played *Las mil y una noches (A Thousand and One Nights)* with Arab princes and princesses, Patricia and a girl who lived at the end of the tall grasses in our neighborhood would take the roles of prince or princess with veils draped across their faces while I—dutifully—played the maid. But Patricia was the sad one. She had a slight curve at the top of her spine, and the doctors worried that it was scoliosis. They ordered a vest with bars made of thin animal bone wrapped in fabric. An exoskeleton. Patricia had to wear this vest inside her clothes. But she never did.

I was busy figuring things out. If mami is sick, she can't help it. Being smart like that gives you fortitude.

Mami

I can almost touch the memory of my mother on that day in the patio under the calabash tree. I must have been in the kitchen when I heard tío Walter's voice, soft and firm, just outside. I stepped out.

Her body is dense and still, like wax. Her eyes don't see me. Mami's beautiful bearing has sunk into itself. I cannot tell if she is listening to my uncle. I don't remember anything I may have said. I was seven. We can see so much when we are seven. We can see everything. Our ears almost hurt; the cells expand to near bursting to reach a point of understanding.

I heard my tío whisper into the phone that morning, "Shock therapy, the sugar kind," he said. "She almost died. Julita almost died." Mami's tongue was strange for weeks. She would stick it out huge and fleshy and pull it back into her mouth. She needed water all the time. My sister and I stayed out of her room until she began to return to normal, but we'd sneak in to borrow scissors or the handheld mirror from her dressing table, knowing we would get away with it. No one said what was wrong. We watched. Patricia and I waited.

For me and Patricia and our baby brother Carlitos, mami was ours, inescapably our *mamá*. She was a piece of us like a nose or budding breasts. When she pressed the fleshy part of her thumb against her teeth—again and again—we were her thumb. "Stop, mami!" we begged.

She turned her head back to talk her anxiety when driving us places, making us crazy afraid of total annihilation in the streets of Panama. She caressed her breasts by sending her fingers into the scoop of her tropical dresses. Patricia and I were mortified when she walked naked and clammy in her bedroom, unconcerned that we were watching. I bit and tore with my teeth any white that I spied at the edge of my nails. Patricia chewed her nails to the quick. We pushed our stumpy fingers into the folds of our skirts.

When mami came to our school, she begged the nuns to pray for her. We were not Catholic, but she sought help from anyone who might have special access. Mami developed any illness that struck a friend or a relative. She relished feeling the pain and demanding the medication.

"Fix yourself up. *Están gordas*. You're fat," she would insist. "What is wrong with you? Why doesn't anyone like you?" The torrent of accusations pushed my sister out of the house, avoiding mami whenever possible. I was sunny, a watcher and a figurer, capable of playing the game.

Mami was sick. *Yo lo sabía.*

I knew it.

"Me odian. Me quieren matar," mami told anyone who would listen. They want to kill me! When she took to her bed in a self-induced illness, I became the emissary between her and the "evil maids." I had the job of bringing meals to her on the white tray with the hinged sides, the hot milk in the Noritake cup, and the English silver setting.

I place the tray down on the bed, and she begins her recitation.

"They want to poison me. They've poisoned the food!"

"Mami, it is not poisoned," I tell her. "I promise, *te juro, te lo juro*, there is no poison. I saw the preparation with my own eyes."

The moment always arrives, *"Entonces pruébalo."* Then taste it! Good little girl that I am, I taste the bitter truth.

I grind a piece of *lomito* with my teeth, and I collect some grains of rice in the cup of my tongue.

Girl

My small heart lifted right out of my chest and floated in front of me like a pretty party balloon, innocent and pink. Papi was home! Papi was home! My sister Patricia also rushed to the door.

"¿Cómo están mis niñas?"

I race my sister to grab the bowl of peanuts for papi, and we tag alongside him on the way to his bedroom. He has a surprise, we know.

He places his briefcase on the bed, unclasps it and pulls out a booklet.

"Here's a new drawing book. Look Marlena!" he says as he points to a page with ears, line drawings of ears. He gives us each a crinkly-sounding cellophane pack with two charcoal sticks.

"Are these charcoals soft?" I ask.

Papi then collapses on the tweedy lounge chair, takes off his shoes, and lifts his feet onto the matching ottoman. There is a round tabletop on the left that sits on a spindly center leg. His glass of scotch and soda is waiting there with ice.

Papi decompresses from a day's work in this chair with a book in his hands. But first he pries off and wipes his gold, wire-rimmed glasses. We know to leave him to his quiet.

Boy

The handsome wand is finished in lustrous dark-brown leather with long, loose, leather straps at one end. Our papi retrieves it from the bedroom. Carlitos is in trouble again.

The father whips his son across the legs and makes him dance. He uses this same strap on his beloved horse, Palomino.

Patricia and I suffer for Carlitos, but we gloat when the beating is inspired by all-out fights with one of us. Stones and spinning tops aimed at our heads.

"*¡El látigo!* You are going to get the whip, just wait!"

"Marlena, *tienes diez centavos?* I'll pay you back. *Te lo prometo. . . .*"

"No Carlitos, no! If I give you a dime for *bombitas*, I know you'll make them burst at my feet." The tiny round explosive bombitas were sold by poor boys on the street. Carlitos threw them hard against the black asphalt under the wheels of passing cars.

Other boys came to our door selling homemade kites. Diamond-shaped kites made with thin colored paper mounted on a cross of *birulí*, a type of bamboo. Carlitos and I attached the right length of tail and released the thick sewing string that was wound on a stick—a little at a time—to feed the kite air, as papi had shown us, without letting it dip. Keep moving. Is that you, Carlitos, flying high? Or is it me?

Dinner

I could hear inside my head. Big chewing sounds. Couldn't others hear this crazy noise? We were all at the table, papi, Carlitos, Patricia, mami—or one of our tías. The long wooden table was set with mats, white, hand-embroidered napkins, silver utensils, and coasters for the sweaty water glasses. The maid came to each of us, quietly presenting a single selection, always from the left. We served ourselves with a large silver spoon. This was difficult for me, being a lefty. I had to squeeze my elbow tight against my ribs. The maid returned the serving plate to the kitchen. If we wanted more, mami would ring the tiny brass bell from Aruba in the shape of a girl.

Mami held herself very straight and chewed her food slowly, feeling with her tongue for little bones in the food if it was fish.

Papi asked us about school. My stories were too long, and I waved my hands about, and I never got to the point. My sister told me to shut up. My father let us not eat something, but if our tía Esther was staying with us when mami was away, we would be forced to swallow the cut up celery in the salad, or the slimy eggplant. My brother hated peas. Tía Esther's insistence, Carlitos's retreat. My father didn't tolerate much of this. "Esther, enough!"

Tía Esther adored her brother, and the quick temper kept her in check.

After finishing our flan or tía Mimí's lemon meringue pie, we played Twenty Questions. Two at a time, we left the table and turned a corner to conspire and think of a really clever thing within a category that no one would ever guess. Things like "a dust particle on Carlitos's eyelash." Or we played *concentración*, thinking really hard about a person and beaming that thought to others at the table. Mami loved this game.

"Begin the Beguine"

My cousin Norma is arriving from England, and mami is planning one of her parties on the terrace.

Norma picks up the lizards by the tail and the wet *sapos,* the toads that serenade us every night, a riotous pulsating sound, they insist, from the beds of earth and bushes that are cut into the brick patio.

Mami and papi plan the balloon-on-the-ankle-of the-woman thing. The man blows up a small balloon and ties it to his partner's ankle. The music starts and everyone is dancing. The men stomp at the back of women's feet. Pop! Everyone laughs.

Mami welcomes guests with a personal question riding on her finest smile. Her glamour is contagious. The food is good: fried sweet root vegetables—*frituras de otoe y yuca frita*—passed by the maids dressed in simple white—with bowls of *chimichurri* sauce for dipping.

At the corner of the covered terrace on the cool ceramic squares is a curved, built-in bar made of *caoba,* one of Panama's abundant mahoganies. Spirits are neatly lined up: gin, rum, and Johnny Walker Scotch, mami's favorite. A sofa and chairs overlook the brick patio three long steps below, the deep yard after that, the pine tree with fragrant needles, and the sugarcane bush. The hammock in the distance reflects the light of the moon.

The entire neighborhood was an expanse of tall spiky grasses—*puro monte*—taller than my little-girl body—when in 1951 mami and papi decided to build their house in Urbanización Obarrio. When the foundation of the house was being laid and after we moved in, we were on the lookout for snakes. *"¡Culebra!"* we shouted with reckless abandon. Our calls alerted the yardman who executed the creatures with the machete he carried strapped to his leg.

Though it was a typical house—stucco walls painted white

with the familiar weave of red clay tiles on the roof—mami and papi built their dream home in inventive ways. The dining table had as a backdrop a long wall of brick next to the sliding glass doors to the terrace. On the brick was a painting of an Indian woman who leaned on a turquoise pillow.

If mami and papi were out for the evening, we would eat at the little pass-through from the kitchen, a narrow rectangular room with its own door to the terrace, a counter and three stools, mesh-covered windows at our backs and toward the howling plants. At every lunch and on many evenings, Patricia, Carlitos, and I ate our simply prepared rice, beef, plantain, and green salad, sometimes a half of *chayote*, hot, with butter on top. Carlitos and I always wound up on the floor of that slice of a room, fighting.

Tonight for the party mami and papi are playing "Begin the Beguine" written by Cole Porter. Mami likes romantic music, her favorite—the Cuban song "Siboney," played very loudly. They are dancing. The thin gold bracelet glistens on her naked ankle.

Mami and papi are the best dancers of their time. The men—all the men—want to dance with Julita.

MATRACA

Navidad

Todo el mundo went to tío Felix's store to buy *juguetes* from the United States and Europe. Even people with very little money who would save for Christmas by putting down one, two, or five dollars per week for twenty-five weeks *en el club de mercancías*. For Carlitos there were clear bags with plastic Indians holding tomahawks and cowboys the color of flesh. *Mis patines* with metal clamps that pinched your toes came from tío Felix's store, also the Faber-Castell colored pencils with shiny cylinders lined up in order. Though we were Jewish, we had a Christmas tree at the front window. But we didn't have a crèche like my friends did. My family traced our ancestors to Spain and Portugal, to Jews who fled to England and Holland after the Spanish Inquisition in 1492. In the 1600s and 1700s they had settled in the Danish, Dutch, and English colonies in the Virgin Islands. Some arrived in Panama in the mid 1800s. When I was growing up, we were a handful of families. Almost all of us were related.

Just before the holiday, after papi came home from work, we would climb into our family car—*el carro de capota*—with the soft black top to buy presents for our cousins. At the top of the Felix list every year were ping pong balls for the table in our open-sided garage, where papi taught us to whack the little white ball to the sharp edges of the wood top and into the bushes with tiny bell flowers that we linked into garlands for our wrists.

Loaded with noisy paper bags and shaking with excitement, we returned to the house to sit on the cool floor of the hall with mami at the telephone table reading our cousins' names and matching them to the presents while we wrapped, our fir tree as tall as the living room ceiling with a star at the top (never an angel).

At dawn on the twenty-fifth—"*¡Apúrate, Patricia!*" —we tip-toed past mami and papi's bedroom and crawled under the low limbs of the tree. Carlitos would already be there. "*¿Encuentras mi nombre?*" we whispered. When we found a tag with our name, we lifted a corner of the wrapping paper until we caught a glimpse of the thing or mystery letters in the box that gave us a clue. Mami's gift was in a tiny package always, a modest piece of jewelry from papi, one time a ring with an oval of jade at the top that she rubbed for luck. To a stranger (there weren't many) she would explain, "It's for my health."

It's a Pain in My Left Arm

"It's a pain in my left arm. *¿Qué me está pasando?*"

Papi would set his hazel eyes on mami and speak softly to calm her. "Honey, you're all right. Please believe me." He said this in English.

"*¡No, me estoy muriendo!*" mami would cry out. "I'm dying!"

The wail could shift without warning into a terrible growl while she squeezed her arm over and over with the other hand.

"The children, think of the children, Julita! You were at the doctor only two weeks ago.

"No!"

"It's in your mind, baby."

"I don't believe you, damn it!"

"You know it well, Julita, that your pains come from unconscious thoughts."

"Damn it!"

This happened on some evenings and would go on for many minutes or for the night. I aimed for the room that I shared with Patricia at the far end of the house. I might come to the front again to spy a little later, my stomach in a knot, and find mami throwing her slippers at papi in the bedroom. If the arguments lasted for hours, papi—his thin lips even thinner—would pronounce, "Julita, I'm taking you to your mother."

I did see a hint of triumph in mami's eyes. She would drop her chin, spent as she was, and she would hush. Then we watched them head outside to the car with mami's small suitcase, leaving for our grandmother's apartment ten minutes from our house.

Even though my English was very halting then, I understood what mami's sister said one afternoon, not knowing that my ears were stretching. "Instead of telling Julita, you have a good man, our mother folds—missing a chance to build her daughter's character." I agreed with my tía, although I didn't say it.

Our grandmother Amamá let mami get away with *todo*!

Loretta Young

She was beautiful—in a Loretta Young kind of way. Long face, high cheekbones, a pointed chin. Mami had deep-set hazel eyes widely placed in her face, nicer eyes than mine. Liquid, like my sister's eyes.

In a bus once, when I may have been eight and she, thirty-one, I saw it. Her hair was medium length with brown waves all around her skin that was lit from the side and had a dreamy surface.

People mentioned the Loretta Young likeness to mami.

"*¿Verdad, me lo juras?*" Mami would ask. "Do you swear it?"

Mami at nineteen or twenty, before she married.

One of my tíos had a very early TV set for the one station beamed at us in Panama from the Canal Zone. We sat in chairs around the small box, five or six of us at a time in the bedroom. If we stopped at his apartment on a Sunday, we would see the jumping acrobats of the Ed Sullivan Show building body pyramids or Sid Caesar's gobbledygook talk in *Your Show of Shows*. I did not need to speak English to know when to laugh at his antics.

The Loretta Young Show happened to us on Wednesdays. In a ravishing gown, Loretta Young stepped leisurely down a long staircase to introduce the story of the week. Her voice was melodious, her carriage impeccable, her gently waved, brown hair a perfect match to mami's. Mami got lost watching her alternate self on the screen. "*¿Verdad?*"

"Shoulders back, stomach in," my mother would recite three or four times every day. She lifted her shoulders up to her ears and rolled them back as she pulled in her belly, which made her chest stick out.

She sat for hours at the *tocador* looking into the mirror, dabbing beige-flesh grease onto her cheeks and forehead, stopping the movement of the tainted rubber sponge to stare into her eyes. She wore body-grazing *trajes de tirita*—round-scooped dresses with thin straps at the shoulders. Or V-necklines to harmonize with the oval of her face. This established a canvas of skin for pearl necklaces and opened a triangular plane for clip-on earrings with fake stones in colors, as was the fashion. Her shoulders and arms were hued warmly from the sun. The bed of her nails was deep, always painted a clear red—clear blood, we imagined, when she plunged the nails into our flesh in crazy moments of panic.

Her anxiety found its locus in the body. "Palpitations"—always feeling for palpitations—had her terrified about a weak heart, an impending attack. I don't know what behavior became so alarming. At what moment papi said, "We can't help Julita here."

In the early 50s mami was taken to Austen Riggs in Stockbridge, Massachusetts. This was a private psychiatric hospital not too distant from her brother Freddy's house in a New York suburb where he lived with his family. When mami could get a weekend reprieve from the hospital, she would visit at tío Freddy's house.

"Shoulders back, stomach in." When my mother made her entrance, she would extend her arms, and with a gleaming smile on crimson lips, she would exclaim, "*¿Cómo están mis amores?*" She asked about her brother's daughters in a glowing, semi-absent way, because she had the good graces and manners of a family who cared about these things. But quickly she would revert to her complaints: "*Mis glándulas*—look they are bulging—the damn doctor won't give me another test." And she would press and poke at her throat and check out her tongue in the mirror, lifting the tongue and all over again.

"Julita with such a fine mind lets this thing take over," commented one of my tías. "It's a lack of self-censorship."

"It's a tragic thing," whispered another.

Matraca

"*Matraca*," Patricia and I would say. A matraca was a small wooden ratchet often used for percussion. It repeated its *clackety* sound as long as you continued to twirl it. Mami, eyebrows pressed together in distress, chased us with questions and disparaging invectives—"What's wrong with me, why doesn't anyone like me?" or "You embarrass me" —right up to the bathroom door where the only solution was to slam and lock the door and pray that after fifteen minutes she would exhaust herself. That it would stop.

During mami's stay at Austin Riggs, my tío Freddy could escape with work and live in the disconnect that my mother's brothers had mastered. My conscientious tía shouldered the burden during these visits. She was the one to attend to the woman with a matraca inside her head that would not stop.

YOUR PAPI IS REALLY YOUR MAMI

Balboa

On Saturday when papi doesn't have work, he grabs the metal box with fishing line and tackle and drives us to avenida Balboa. We go early before anyone is up, though it is bright and already hot. Parque Urraca is across the avenue with the white gazebo and the seesaw, but we've come to fish.

Papi parks on the half circle surrounding the statue, and we walk a few feet to the break in the wall that holds back the craggy ocean. It's low tide. If you get close enough, you can pick up a whiff of fishiness and a dull, sweet, not unpleasant smell. The sewers spill into this water that borders the city.

Papi brings bait and gives Carlitos and me a line that he helps cast into the water past the rocky edge. We crouch and wait. Behind us—way above our heads—is Vasco Núñez de Balboa: shiny brown, feet on the marble sphere of the world, dressed in the armor of the conquistadores. Our city's hero has planted a bronze flag of Spain on the world, and with his right hand he raises the bottom end of his sword that looks like a cross up to the sky. Indian guides have taken our hero to a peak where he views this miracle. "I've discovered a new ocean, and I will call it *mar del sur*," which in relation to my country that curves west to east is in the south.

Magellan years later will call the new ocean "Mar Pacífico."

Papi played *fútbol* with us and with our friends in the backyard, also *béisbol* with hard rubber balls that I could hit. Sometimes our friends lined up for a simple catch. If you dropped the ball, you were a toad, a *sapo,* and had to get out of the line.

"¡Sapo!"

Patricia, Carlitos, and I spent Saturday afternoons with papi planting *crotos* and raking needles from under the old pine tree.

The croto shrubs ringed our house in reckless color.

They gorged on the heat.

Sunday

On Sundays we swam at the El Panamá, the first luxury hotel in our city, designed by the American architect Edward Durrell Stone and finished in 1952. The eight-story building looked like an envelope set on its long edge on a grassy hill. Chalk white on top of green, and blue sky everywhere.

Patricia, Carlitos, and I swam in the Olympic-size pool, surrounded by cabanas and leafy banana plants, until we were prunes and stank of chlorine, in spite of our shower before ice cream cones at the end of the afternoon. *Un barquillo* with a giant scoop of vanilla!

"*Cinco centavos, señorita.*"

*

"Carlitos is a fish," papi said, "but he needs technique." When he wasn't doing drills with Carlitos in the water, papi would be playing at the ping-pong table or having a Scotch with a friend. He looked lonely without mami.

Patricia liked to pretend she was Esther Williams, leaning on one foot at the curvy rim of the pool. I watched her when I wasn't busy being me. Because I am what Patricia is not. Patricia holds things in. I tend to spill them out. Same water down from the mountain. We are sister rivers.

I loved to jump and bomb into the water from the small diving board. The tall one was scary and inevitable. You climbed twelve narrow metal steps and walked onto the flexible plank. The side rails stopped suddenly, and you were on your own. It would be embarrassing to climb down. People would see the backs of my doughy legs again, on the steps. No, no, not that.

Hold your nose, keep your feet together, and pray. Okay, okay. . . .

"¡Apúrate. Marlena!"

Okay, I'm gonna go. ¡Qué miedo! It looks so much higher from here, as if I am at the top of the white envelope.

Have to do it. Here I go. Jump!

I pull one last gasp of air, and I plunge down hard into the water.

Drive-in

After he pays the car charge of un dolar setenti-cinco, papi drives into the grassy field and picks a spot in between two short posts. He pulls in, lifts the boxy metal speaker from the stand, and clamps it loosely over his door. We hear the awful sounds of static, *cri cri cri*. This crunchy music confirms deliciously that we are at the *auto cine*. In the breeze, under the big open sky, at the drive-in.

Every Friday night we pile up into our carro de capota. We are clad in our pajamas, ready to drop off into slumber and be carried into our beds when papi drives us home after the movie.

"Who is that?" Patricia points to a car two cars down on the right. "Is that Marcelita with her brother?"

"Marcelita, come and sit with us!"

We sink back into the seats. The screen is lit! Floating up there, giant, in VistaVision, like the moon except that it is almost square. There it is in the emptiness, sky upon sky. A lone horse is riding over the empty mesa.

A young man sets a tray over the passenger side door. *"Buenas noches, we have jot dogs y papas con mostaza, Coca, Orange Crosh, y soda de uva."*

"Un jot dog para mí y uno para Poli." Carlitos wants a hot dog and one for his best friend Poli. And he wants the potato fries with honey that we love.

If there are not too many cars, papi lets us sit on top of the back to be higher even on the sky of the world.

Marcelita says, "Your papi is really your mami."

GALAXY

Vicks VapoRub

I am not going to school today. How delicious it is to be sick. Amamá is certain to come.

"How are you, *mi querida*? Let me check your forehead. Are you coughing much?"

Amamá—*mi abuela*— administers the magic potion, Vicks VapoRub, the favored remedy. She spreads the unguent on my back and on my chest. I feel delightfully cool under her tender hands. She dabs some Vicks paste into my nostrils, a little more bracing. If she feels truly magnanimous, I get to swallow a clot of the ointment, like downing a dab of glue.

She brings me *cómicas* and books of *maricas*, paper dolls with punch-out skirts, hats, and hockey sticks. Amamá stays with me for a long time.

Amamá worries about mami.

La Cigüeña/The Stork

La cigüeña began its descent looking for the spiny bit of land lapped on two sides by the tides. It knew to drop me in the slender corridor that linked the mass of land in the north to the one in the south, holding steady between the scoops of two powerful oceans.

As she approached, she worried about the recurring problem of leaving a human in the arms of an uncertain mother, but as she reached the lush green zone and scanned the land below tree level, she saw the sturdy white sheet underneath the mother, a hundred fingers gripping it tightly along the edges, holding it taut.

La cigüeña decided.

Sisters

I knew them in the times of sagging breasts inside loose brassieres, in the times of purple-washed hair. My Amamá is not a beauty; the wide cheekbones slope rapidly into a downy chin. Her eyes are the draw. Blue and melting into feeling.

Amamá and two of her sisters were widowed early. Amamá with seven children. Tía Emily with four. Tía Anita, only twenty-two when she lost her husband—felled by a carbuncle—two babies to tend to, an infant still in her *entrañas*. When I was a girl in the 1950s and 60s, the three sisters held court in the El Madurito, the apartment building that my uncles had designed and built in the new neighborhood of El Cangrejo. Amamá and tía Anita lived in 1A and Emily in 2A, though Emily was always *pasando el tiempo* with her sisters. They sat in the breezy living room: Emily recounting tales of thieves under her bed, Amamá knitting baby booties, Anita fashioning children's dresses threaded with blue and pink satin ribbon.

El Madurito was the freshest place to be in the hot city. As tall as eight stories and built catty-corner on the property, the building emboldened the air currents, invited them into the open balconies, and helped them escape via precisely positioned windows.

I knew that when I went to 1A, I would find cousins and playmates, but I had to plot my arrival. How to avoid kissing the grannies?

Tía Anita with the bluest hair sat closest to the open balcony in the rocking chair. Tía Emily sat on the green armchair, Amamá on the couch. I entered the apartment through the kitchen, complicit with Juanita, the laughing cook. I snuck in a peek. If I was lucky, one or all three would be nodding, chins dropping into their chests, snoring in syncopation. When I got my chance, I would advance nonchalantly across the common hall to the bedrooms. Almost always I was caught.

"*¿Por qué no vienes a saludar?*" Amamá would look at me sternly and aim her cheek toward her sisters indicating the proper placement of duty. Then, with a worried look she would say, "You look pale. Go and put on a little *colorete,* a little rouge," when I was nine. *Ser bonita,* being beautiful, was todo.

"*¡Patricia! ¡No salgas sin tus aretes!*"

An acute body consciousness was the inadvertent gift of a loving family.

Her son Arturo had to be like his cousin Stanley. Carlitos had to be Dito. Everyone was not quite right being themselves.

Some came to Apartment 1A to perch, some came for gossip, and others came to eat—chauffeurs, old *nanas* from the past—anyone who was hungry. A little bit of meat was stretched with rice and vegetables and soup. No one left with an empty belly. Several of

Amamá's sons with their wives and children lived in the building. Tío Mikey lived in 1C, tío Walter in 4, tío Freddy (later) in 5, tío Arturo in 7. Amamá's brother George lived in 5. All stopped by to kiss Amamá before leaving for work, or to have lunch at noon with mother, or to unwind at the end of the day.

Babies, old and new babies, were brought to be kissed and held.

Everyone knew that mami was Amamá's favorite, the baby daughter who demanded so much. If Patricia and I said anything about mami, Amamá's index finger would jump to the edge of her teeth where she would pin it tightly, willing the walls not to listen.

My favorite meal at Amamá's was hot okra soup with a chunk of fungi—a cornmeal concoction, specialty of St. Thomas—bread-thins very slowly brought to a crisp in the oven, and coffee dripped through a white sock into a cooking pot.

A Small Star

There was one small commercial unit on the ground floor of the El Madurito, and I went with Amamá every few weeks, and all my cousins had their haircuts there too. Charles was Italian. He must have thought the name "Charles" fitted a hairdresser instead of Carlo or Giuseppe. We said "Charrles" extending the "r" sound. To us he was glamorous when he spoke his medley of Spanish-Italian and held the cutting scissors with the pinkie finger sticking out. But I never came out looking glamorous. My medium thick, dark brown hair was cut medium short and always looked the same with *picos* or wings on the sides of my face. Charles thought my long face deserved this widening and that's what I got every time. I was okay: medium family good looks on fair skin—cheekbones, pretty skin, good teeth. My wrists and ankles were thin like Patricia's, and I wasn't so much shorter than *mis primas*, my cousins, who were medium in height. The family resemblance almost blended. We were all cut from the same bolt.

I was a small star in the galaxy of family. We traveled in *pandillas*, little gangs that reconfigured for a cooling movie *el domingo* or a party, or tea at the house of one of our *tías*, *comparsas* at *carnaval*, and hanging around in the heat. We learned to ignore the bossy one, or choke down a mean remark, or swoon over the beauty. We were docile, following exactly the rules of etiquette and respect for elders, prefacing all requests with a *por favor* and following most with a *gracias*, stopping to listen to a reproving aunt or to laugh at an uncle's *chistes,* bound together in comforting clusters. Certain that none of us would fall out.

Padrino

Tío Walter cut down tall grasses in the countryside and built a house next to a virgin beach three hours from the city. Panama City, which was the capital, housed most of the people in Panama. Other than Colón on the Atlantic side and David, close to Costa Rica, the rest of the country was dotted with small, rural towns and jungle. The road along the countryside was paved roughly, and even in the dry season, we saw miles of stumpy wood fences with clumps of leaves pushing out at the tops of the desiccated wood.

Papi bought blocks of ice for the ice chest. Mami would insist we stop halfway for *bollos,* cornmeal—hot—wrapped in corn husks, from a family who owned a stand of white cement block with a sheet of corrugated metal on top. As we got close to tío Walter's place, the main road turned toward the ocean and bent to the right to fit three dwellings. Tío Walter and tía Betty's white stucco house with its dark wooden door barely held back the bush.

In spite of the screened windows, we had to poke under the mattress before making our bed when we arrived, to alert others with a piercing scream that a scorpion had been sighted. We lit small coils, believing that the heady, burning fumes would keep mosquitoes at bay. Cloti taped flypaper to the kitchen ceiling.

We showered warily, one eye searching the dark corners of the tiny stalls for still, wet cockroaches and alarming spiders. We sat on pillows on the floor listening to scary spirit tales embellished by our long-legged and darkly wacky tía Betty. Once a ravishing English beauty, tía Betty sucked us easily into her labyrinth of spooks. At night we slept to the heartbeat of the tides and to the rustle of ghosts.

This was tío Walter's place, set high overlooking the Pacific Ocean, palm trees on the crest. Broken cement steps scrambled to the water. A sea of wiry orange crabs parted and vanished as we approached.

El río at the end of a twenty-minute walk, the river merging into the sea in the heat of the noonday sun.

Cooling off in the tepid water, crashing waves filling our swimsuits with sand and pulling back into the infinite sea.

We swam in the pool of rocks. We rested on the hammocks in the windy ridge of the hill, bellies full of rice and meat.

Mami's brother, tío Walter, had been handpicked for me by my mother to be my *padrino*. Even though he had his own children, I felt that tío Walter, my godfather, belonged to me. Tío Walter looked at you carefully and cocked his head, distracted by other thoughts at the very moment that he paid attention. Mami's other brothers had this dimension of full-hearted emotion, a self-pleasuring love of life, multicolored like the fan of a *pavo real*, a peacock suddenly appearing in the wild and spreading its tail to make us gaze in rapture.

"Walter had a nervous breakdown when he was young," I had heard the gossip.

"He followed Meher Baba, an Indian God-man who didn't talk for forty-four years."

"Walter was swept into something he couldn't control."

These stories made my tío mysterious and explained the guru-like calmness that I sensed about him, though he was not free of the family's prodigal vanity.

Mi padrino massaged his receding hairline, fingers moving to nudge the follicles along.

My not-so-tall padrino was silent much of the time. He stretched with yoga movements on the hot beach where you had to be close to the lapping water so as not to burn your feet. Run run run across the burning black sand to get to the wet. He bent down if he saw a dried log with an unusual shape. At the house he placed the wood on a table to enjoy the specimen of nature death. He built an arbor of metal wire where he hung a yard-full of earth buckets, orchids in unison blotting out the sun.

Tío Walter employed Cloti, a local woman, to work in the house, and he talked to her like a friend. He was intrigued by Cloti, as he was by everything, as he was by mami's illness. When mami needed him, tío Walter assumed the responsibility for mami's psychiatric care. He discussed treatment with the doctors. He picked up mami when it was time for her to return home from

My baby naming dress—that papi also wore in his time—
was influenced by Catholic and European traditions.

hospitals in the United States. Tío Walter could live with the slight
aberration of mami.

Las Mañanitas

At four in the morning every February fourth, tío Mikey would
croon with his trio of guitarists on the lawn of the El Madurito,
next to the walks and the hair salon and the palm trees underneath the balcony of apartment 1A. It is Amamá's birthday. Any
grandchild and thereafter any great-grandchild will plan to be
here. We sleep in the bedrooms wherever we can find a narrow
place next to another in a bed or on the floor under a sheet.

The sliding door to the balcony is left open, and we hear the
first notes. We congregate at the balcony with Amamá who is
wearing Mikimoto pearls on top of her crisscross robe. We sing
along with tío Mikey:

Estas son las mañanitas que cantaba el rey David
a las muchachas bonitas, te las cantamos a ti.
Despierta mi bien despierta,
mirá que ya amaneció
que los pajaritos cantan
la luna ya se ocultó

These are the morning serenades that King David sang
to the pretty maidens, and we sing them to you.
Awaken, my treasure, awaken
See, it is dawn!
The little birds are singing
The moon has already hid.

GOLDILOCKS

Goldilocks

Goldilocks found the pretty house built on a hill. It was hot outside, and she had to climb twenty-seven steps to reach the large front door made of wood. The walls of the house were stucco white with nice big stones stuck here and there; the roof tiles were red. Goldilocks pushed the heavy door, but it wouldn't budge.

Someone heard her.

"*¡Hola Manenín!* Who brought you?" Tía Connie smiled and kissed me on the cheek, and then she turned her head back and called out, "Margie, Margie, Manenín is here."

The Mama Bear was home. Her eyes had love, and her voice was high and slightly breathless, as if the roof were going to cave in at any moment. Papa Bear was at the office. The three little bears—there were three baby bears, not one—were in different parts of the house. One was in the back room tinkering with the piano and the two youngest were fighting in the bedroom. Goldilocks walked toward the crazy sounds of girl bears at war. She entered a long bedroom with three matching beds all in a row.

The beds were covered with pink chenille spreads that had little puffy balls of cotton all over.

Margie was on top of her baby sister, Linky, and biting her hard on the arm. Linky was yanking on Margie's thick blond hair. Already there were small clumps of hair on the bed.

"*¿Qué pasa? ¿Qué pasa?* What are you doing?" Tía Connie runs into the bedroom beside herself, screaming. "Stop! Margie, leave your sister alone."

One more yank and one last sink of teeth before they stop. Margie gets up and walks off in a huff. Baby bear tells her mami, "*Margie comenzó*, she started it. *¡Ella comenzó!*"

More rarely my older cousin Gay is involved, and she fights, too, with every tool in her body arsenal: fingers for pinching, nails and teeth for digging, fists for pounding, legs for pinning down, words to incite. I watch, fascinated. The older bears get the blame. The baby bear who started the excitement walks off, clutching Mama Bear's hand.

Margie and I were just one year apart. We called each other "*hermanita*," little sister. My little sister followed a thought, picking at it and picking at it; her excitement was contagious. I stayed at Margie's house almost half of my life. I was safely inside, and I looked longingly into the window.

All five were beautiful. Fairy-tale perfect. Margie's father tío Stanley, who rode horses with papi, was tall, quiet, and handsome, a non-fumbling Clark Kent. A man to make decisions. A man you can rely on to be cool and fair. Tío Stanley was in business, but his instincts were progressive, as suited his degree in psychology from Stanford in the era of John Dewey. Tía Connie was his foil, appropriately emotional. Tía Connie wore her feelings on her sleeve. She was a good cook and a devoted mother. The girls had the mother's oval face set into well-defined facial architecture and the refinement of the father's features, long straight eyelashes, almond eyes, and slender noses. Margie was fair and blonde. Though she was one year younger than me, Margie had developed early and had an hourglass figure. A doll's face on a woman's body. I was a regular girl with a baby-fat belly, near invisible to the boys pining for mi hermanita, An ache for myself was eased by my own devotion to Margie. Her life and mine were woven neatly. I got a generous piece of Mama and Papa Bear and the house on the hill.

Our families spoke English well, though the children were raised in Spanish. In the islands of the West Indies where earlier generations of my family had lived, English was the language of trade. I honed my English on tía Connie's love comics. In *True Romance* I cried over the man who got away. "Does he love me? How shall I tell him the truth?" This was my English. Traditional family values for the little woman at home.

The house on the hill was crammed with comic books. Love, and Archie, Betty and Veronica. Little Lulu kept me company. I curled up on top of the chenille spread with the puffy dots and disappeared. "*Manenín está en la luna.*" Marlena's on the moon. Learning English with Dagwood.

SKIN

Sweet Tarts

"You'll grow up to be old maids like your aunts," mami sang to Patricia and me.

"Julita doesn't appreciate your wonderful papi," they refrained. "Your mami is spoiled," they said. "She doesn't deserve him."

Mami would leave Panama two times for lengthy stays in mental hospitals in the United States when I was a girl.

Not fully with the rights of a mother, my father's two sisters became surrogates for mami when mami had to travel for treatment. One or the other would sleep at our house and manage the household to help their brother, Eddie. My father's two sisters never married.

My favorite—tía Mimí—was lumpy. With dark brown hair and eyes like mine, she had little bumps all over her body and her face. Most were no bigger than a pearl. Some grew to the size of marbles. They floated under her skin. I felt their softness when I held her hand. This was how she was, and no one talked about it.

My tía Esther was fat. Whiter than her sister with blue, luminous eyes, she wore loose turquoise and pink dresses that landed below her fleshy knees, with a pliable fabric belt made in the cloth of the dress.

My tías lived in a modest apartment on the second floor that pulled a good breeze through the ironwork and thin metal screens at the front, the curio cabinet, and out the kitchen window at the back. Tía Mimí had a rectangular table of cool, white metal where she rolled the famous dough. Unlike other white women of her class, she worked.

"Secretive like a Mason," mami used to say, tía Mimí poured her heart into pastries that she made at home and sold to mothers and wives for their parties.

I learned to roll pastry with tía Mimí, to cut circles with the open end of a glass, and to lift the perfect moons and place them— without pressing much—into the tiny metal pans. I dropped a petite dollop of prune or pineapple or guava mixture into the center of each pan. Tía Mimí would let me use the wavy rolling wheel to cut thin strips of remaining dough and place an "x" over the filled pans. I dipped the tip of a fork into icy water and pressed the edges of the strips to link them to the dough underneath.

We filled large rectangular baking trays with rows and rows of the little tarts. Two pans at a time, tía Mimí bent down and placed them into the preheated oven. She knew exactly when they would be ready, but she always checked. When we sat at the table at the end of the afternoon, tía Mimí would let me suck on the tangy pulp of tamarind seeds that we picked from the tree outside at the back. The sweet and sour sensation twisted my mouth in wincing delight.

Tía Esther studied nursing and became an RN, "¡No una práctica!" she insisted, wagging her finger at us. Tía Esther took care of other women's babies at the hospital, accompanying the families home after the birth and taking care of children when their parents traveled. She was one of them—white people could trust her. Though tía Esther saw herself belonging to two distinct worlds, collecting old clothes and money for "*mi gente*," the mestizo maids and ordinary people she encountered in the humble circles of her nursing work.

Tía Esther pierced our buttocks with the sharp points of medicinal syringes. She checked our throat with the thick *paleta* that tasted vaguely of orange as it pressed on our tongue and made us gag. "Never drink from someone else's glass or take a bite of their fruit," she warned us. "Don't borrow panties from your friends and cousins," she whispered.

My tías kept hundreds of tiny figurines inside a four-tier wooden cabinet with glass sides and shelves. They were the size of a fingernail or a single joint of a finger, maybe two, objects collected during tía Esther's travels with her nursing colleagues or brought by friends who knew of their cupboard. Diminutive people in porcelain, plastic, glass, and wood from Guatemala, Holland, Venice, Japan, Spain. Plates, forks, spoons, pies, cakes, washing board, easel with dots for paint, combs, shoes, dolls with tiny feet. Carlitos, his small back curved like a "c," could be still for hours, squinting his eyes, spellbound. Cowboy boots, watermelons, bananas, guavas, pineapples, chocolates with a cherry in a box, boy with marching drum, sailboats, airplanes, helicopter, horse, birds, snakes, dogs, cats, frog, donkey, kite, sling, beach ball, baseball, bat.

Tía Mimí was just as proud of their treasures, although she never said an extra word. Tía Esther chose to work with noisy babies. Tía Mimí, with tools and precise, sweetened food, everything encased in pastry, even the savory.

We saw tía Mimí push her younger sister with quiet.

Sometimes we heard them fight like cats.

Tía Esther picked my sister, the first-born, as her pet. "Patricia, *mi preferida*." The breath got caught in my chest every time. When she got excited, tía Esther's voice would start high and break into miniature chirps, like the *periquitos* that my tías kept in a white cage next to the curio cabinet. When we heard this sound we knew there would be presents. One Christmas, tía Esther's high-pitched call signaled something special, and we ran to the balcony where she was standing. There was a smile on her face. She was clutching her purse. When the three of us were properly attentive, tía Esther twisted the snap of her purse with a flourish. She pulled out three thin booklets, each in a blue paper sleeve.

"Here's Patricia's." Tía Esther slid one of the books from its sleeve. "See her name here? These are bankbooks. See the number five? I've put in five dollars for Patricia and for each of you. Every Christmas I will deposit another five; this will teach you about saving."

From a drawer in her bedroom tía Esther pulled out a large cardboard box. She lifted the top and spread the white tissue to show us a beautiful *pollera*. I touched the white embroidered flounces of the festive dress. "You'll get it dirty, Marlena." She held up a smaller box full of the loopy, beaded ornaments that a girl wearing a pollera would pin on her hair. She lifted a *cadena chata*, a long necklace, the metal parts flattened. "This one is real gold . . . *de oro.* This is *my* pollera made by the best artisans in the country-side. It's for Patricia when she turns thirteen."

Tía Esther unveiled the silver pieces that belonged to "my side of the family, your father's side."

Tía Mimí, not so showy, became mine by reduction.

Tía Esther tried to console me with empty words, "Marlena, you take no nonsense from your mother."

You belong to your mother. This is what tía Esther really meant. It made me want to defend mami.

"Don't say that, tía Esther."

Oye Carlitos

"*Oye Carlitos*, what happened to you yesterday?" tía Mimí prompted slyly, knowing the comedic story that would embarrass him. Carlitos's deep blush shamed me, even as I took part in the game. His friend Ricardito completed the story.

Tía Esther wearing the pollera that she loved.

"Carlitos was running naked and he fell into the cesspool!"

"*Ayayay, ayayay,*" we all screamed, squirming at the thought of greasy feces sticking to our bodies.

Carlitos was shaky still because when streaking across the lush yard he had fallen into the filthy pool that was normally covered by a thick cement slab about two feet square.

"*¿Y quién te sacó, Carlitos?*" my tía continued. My aunts loved to tease him; what did they know about raising a boy?

Carlitos is a little boy on a pony alongside papi on his horse, Palomino. Carlitos, with a big cowboy hat over his pencil-narrow head, is so slight that the ponies are always chewing down on the grass, the soft-rope *bozales* no challenge to their habits. Carlitos extends his arms taut to pull up the horse's head while papi moves on to the jumps, holding his arms straight out when he takes flight.

Me!

It wasn't mami who took us to Regina cradling a thick fold of fabric to have our dresses made. That was tía Esther.

Tía Esther, fresh in her pink puffy skin, squeezed between the tubes of cloth that leaned crazily into the street in the sweltering *tiendas de tela* on avenida Central. She thumbed through packets of dress patterns cut by Vogue or McCall's held loosely in boxes, bodice and skirt quarters printed on thin yellow paper with skipping lines and dots for the pins when making *pinzas* under the bust (if you had a bust).

Regina, her pockmarked face next to my face, measured *la talla,* holding the soft yellow tape at the center of my shoulder line, drawing it down to my waist. Regina, who may have been from

El Salvador, pinned the puzzle of sheer pattern pieces around me and cut the shoulder if it was too wide or added a slice of newspaper to make the skirt wider. I liked to feel the cold, curved edge of the scissors pressing against my skin when Regina cut a scoop around my neckline, dragging it on my chest and along my back. This was me.

Our guitar teacher was serious and proper in his all-beige suit even though it was hot, his face and hands a yellowish dark as he puffed on a cigar. He may have been Cuban. He spent our class time sliding his flat finger over the chords, making us swoon at his music, plucking with his right on the strings of a classical guitar. It was papi who organized this. I could hurl a flamenco song in a strong pure voice, *Granada* or *La Virgen de La Macarena* played at every bullfight, but I had no aptitude for the difficult work of pressing the plastic strings and denting my fingers red at the top of the guitar.

Skin

So I push a new wave of yellow skin with my thumbs when I give mami her massage. I pull in my breath to send strength to my fingers that catch on the silky straps of her gown. The skin mingles with the drooping gown. Mami is lying facedown on the big bed, almost naked. Her face is turned to the louvered window, and her right arm is twisted backwards. The red fingernails scrape little arcs on my knee. Today mami is a witch. If I don't think or breathe, I will disappear. Her flesh is clammy. It's always clammy. There are specks of black on the top of her shoulders, "my freckles," she remembers, as I press on them to send the muscle down. Her mouth is loose. In a few moments she will let out a snore that will startle me.

Shall I leave? Instead, I stare at the vials of yellow pills on the night table. I check the flesh on my own chewed fingers. I can give "*un masaje delicioso,*" mami says. I know it's true. I also know that I am not mami. Why do I know this? Because I am not nervous. Because I work at lining up my thoughts.

Mami talks about her body all the time. Her mushy lungs and cancer or a lump on her *teta* or the muscle of her pumping heart or her ear-shaped kidneys or her scary tongue and the painted skin. It's mami's body against me.

Swimming Pool

I was ten. My birthday cake was a sky-blue swimming pool, deep and exciting, surrounded by a green, shredded-coconut lawn. There were people under umbrellas in the green expanse, and over the pool a trampoline with a girl perched on top. Tía Mimí made this cake as she made all of our birthday cakes. I cut into the tasty yellow sponge, two layers made in 10x18 pans spread with coffee filling not too sweet. And I made a wish.

WHOSE CRAZY GENES?

The First Julita

"Julita," with a Spanish "jota" sounding like a "who." Whoo-leetah.

My great-grandmother Julita—she was born Judith—lived with my great-grandfather Isidore in Panama City in an attached house on calle Sexta on the second story, reached by a wood staircase that arrived onto a spacious front parlor. Every afternoon all the cousins knew that they were welcome at Julita's for tea and company.

The silver was gleaming. There were cakes and biscuits set out by Machí, the maid from Jamaica who prepared tremendous lunches to fill the bellies of the eight grandchildren now living at Julita's house. The eldest, Felipito, would break for lunch after pumping gas by the railroad tracks, Bobby after peddling Clover Blossom Butter from house to house in the old city. It was the early 1900s.

No ham at meals, no shellfish, like proper Jews. *Sopa* to start always. Herring salad or codfish balls. A serving of meat, vegetable, *yuca*, *plátano*, and papaya served with a demitasse of strong coffee.

Teatime was an excellent occasion for matchmaking ventures. Julita was renowned for her prowess in this respect. Especially, she prepared the girls. She established inevitable facts with the might of her flashing blue eyes. "In marriage the woman is everything. The man," she instructed, "is only a means to an end." Beyond assuring the right mate for her own daughters and the nieces and nephews in Panama, Julita would seek out young relatives on the island of St. Thomas, in Curacao and Jamaica, in Hamburg, Amsterdam, London, and Bordeaux. There were kin—good clay to work with—in the Caribbean and in the old country.

The small Panama clan of my great-grandmother's time met for prayers on plaza de la Catedral near droguería Preciado, on a small street up some steps from a woodworking shop. The room was fitted with benches, and Isidore's brother Moi led the service. Isidore had started an electrical goods shop in Panama, selling lamps and electric fans. Their father had been a rabbi on the island of St. Thomas. Spanish-Portuguese settlers in Panama would not have a rabbi for at least fifty years.

My great-grandfather Isidore, with his thick mustache and white suits, was gentle and beloved. When he was sick he would beseech, "Please, don't tell the doctor what I'm feeling." Clearly, Julita ruled the roost. She was regarded as the matriarch of her generation. I never met my great-grandmother who died years before I was born. She is linked to me by that beautiful name that also belongs to my mother.

While the first Julita was learned and open to ideas, the generation that followed could not match her in confidence and grit. When three of her daughters were widowed, Julita held as their backbone. My grandmother, Amamá, relied on her mamá to manage the children and make decisions. The pattern would persist for another generation. *My* Julita—*my* precocious mami—learned her lessons well. When there is a problem, call on mother to fix it.

Madurito

The ladies at the store spray perfume inside the fold in my arms, and they smudge little dabs of colorete on my cheeks. I visit with Amamá almost every Saturday morning. Mami will be busy at the hairdresser. We drive all the way from Bella Vista to avenida Central, the main commercial street of the city. Short side streets that link to the avenue are crammed with stalls selling earrings and dresses and pots. It's hot hot hot, though inside Madurito, the air conditioning moves the hairs on my arm y *tengo los pelos de punta*. The salesladies, who are mostly white, say, *"¿Cómo está doña?"* with a lilt to their voices. They linger with Amamá as she peers into the glass displays and asks a question about the Noritake dishes or the cultured pearls from Japan. Amamá owns the store—along with her sons who inherited the business from their father Jicky. I watch Amamá lift her chin as she talks to the ladies in a kind of supplication.

The photo of my grandfather Jicky has a special place in the store. "Madurito" they called him. He stares into the camera like a little Caruso dressed in three pieces of grey.

When I'm bored at the store, I cross the side street perpendicular to avenida Central and walk into Café Durán. I make a beeline for the glass vat in the corner where the coffee beans are ground. With my nose pressed on the glass I watch the copper dust fly. This will last one minute. The coffee perfume will jam into my head, driving me back to Madurito to wait while Amamá murmurs her goodbyes.

I touch her soft, freckled hand. Amamá doesn't rush, but she's heading out the glass door into the heat. My heart is swelling. It almost hurts to love her.

In the car at noon, my head feels like it will explode from the heat.

Is Jicky the One?

"Is he the one?" Patricia and I sometimes said. "Is Jicky the reason why mami is sick?"

His grandchildren liked to hear the stories. Tales of séances that our grandfather Jicky—who was born in 1879 and died in 1931—held with tío "Abrúm," Abraham, married to tía Adela. The men listened for sounds of rappings and tappings . . . hands divining over a three-legged stool that had no nails. Once in the dark a young man's voice called out: "I've died in war, and my family doesn't know where I am buried." The soldier's voice asked that his parents who lived in New Jersey be called. Jicky phoned a cousin in New York. "Please look up the family; they need to be told."

Tía Evy, Jicky's eldest daughter, said, "He wanted the best and the biggest! Always an exaggeration! He lost large sums of money and had to be rescued by family."

Before he met Amamá, Jicky opened several *cantinas* near construction sites for the new American canal begun in 1904 after Panama became independent from Colombia in 1903. Jicky had owned a photography studio in Colón, Panama's second city, and painted watercolor seascapes. He recorded with his camera things that no one had witnessed before. Mountains were being carved at his doorstep; lakes were invented. Jicky was the artist behind many of the postcards and souvenir books that he sold.

"Finest Selection of Choice Panama Hats for Ladies and Gentlemen." I.L.Maduro—Jicky's store—was on the corner of plaza de la Catedral in the old city. There were shelves on all sides stacked with hats, fine-woven straw hats that he imported from a cousin in Ecuador and sold to men working the canal or making the crossing of the isthmus.

Mi abuelo's postcard and calling card. Panama Hats floating down a man-made valley that cuts through the continental divide.

"When Albert Einstein traveled to Panama for a ceremonial crossing of the new canal, *tu abuelo* gave the physicist his first Panama hat," my older cousins said.

Jicky carried maps, books, fishing tackle, egret feathers, ostrich eggs, shrunken heads, and women's underthings from Paris. He sold small rocks, polished souvenirs of canal construction (that he imported from Germany). During carnaval he added confetti and *serpentina* to his stock, for the tourists hanging out on the balconies of the Hotel Central over the plaza.

It was still standing when I was a girl, the storybook house that Jicky built in 1915 in Bella Vista. He had been one of the first to settle in the new neighborhood outside the colonial city of Panama. The house was a miniature castle set high on a mound. It had a queenly turret and long white balconies like ribbons that laced against the undulating walls. My grandfather had fallen in love with the prototype during a visit to Germany. He copied it against a backdrop of coconut and mango trees and planted twisting pumpkin vines leading to the house.

After Jicky moved to Bella Vista with Amamá and their four children, he invited Anita—Amamá's widowed sister—and her three children to live with them. Mami was born in the house in Bella Vista. With seven of their own plus Anita's three, the house was wild with children.

"Jicky loved to tease me," Amamá confided. "When screaming children had me threatening horrible punishments, Jicky would call out, 'Essie, which one shall I flush first?' and then *yo me calmaba.* I could relax." Gentle and forgiving, mi abuelo never punished the children. He rocked in his rocker, oblivious, and he heard everything.

Jicky outfitted a lush garden—with the assist of Clarence, *el jardinero*—and he built a life-sized playhouse at the back. There were birds everywhere—we heard this from tía Inés who had lived in the house just behind. Eight canaries in the balcony. Parakeets eating from Jicky's plate. *Guacamayas* screeching inside the trees.

Jicky and Amamá's storybook house in Bella Vista; with so much family, the house was always filled with children.

After his move to Bella Vista, Jicky would drive into the old city with his youngest son Arturo who polished and polished the car while his father lost and lost at poker at the Hotel Central on plaza de la Catedral.

"Jicky *era un soñador* . . . he was a dreamer. . . ."

"Jicky took to his bed for weeks in despair."

Was Jicky the culprit, the one we could blame for mami? Some primos and tíos had periods of depression—or they overflowed with emotion. People said the "crazy" parts came from the de Castro family blood in Jicky's and in all of our lines.

Everyone was related, first cousins married to first cousins, all the qualities remixing. Some appearing to thicken as they doubled up.

Cousins

Pretty, pretty girls, ripe as grapes, loving fun, seeking attention, both a little anxious as became the family. Mami and her first cousin Connie were destined for one another by their sex, surrounded as they were by boy children: my mother's five brothers, Connie's one, and the five Motta boys, sons of Amamá's sister Emily. All gathered at their grandmother's house on calle Sexta in the old city.

They came to visit on November 3, *el Día de la Independencia*, to watch the marchers drumming on the central plaza. In February they could count on the pleasurable little frights brought on by the pouncing *diablitos* in paper maché masks pleading, "*Un real y bailo*," announcing the start of carnaval. On Friday nights they came for evening prayers read from the old Orthodox prayer book at the matriarch's house.

The two cousins also played together at young Julita's house in Bella Vista in the large garden full of birds and in the life-sized playhouse at the back that had its own balcony and windows. All the primos hid to Julita's favorite version of the tag game, *el tuntún de la caravela*. If you were tagged you became the haunting ghost and could spook the others in a gravely voice, "*el tuntún de la caravela*."

Connie and Julita were good girls. It was their one option. Select all from the following: Be beautiful, and, if you can't be that, have *gracia*. Assist this with frills and bows and paint. Be *dulce*, be sweet, have *buenas maneras, contesta bonito,* sonríe. Kiss los tíos, have *amigas.* Find a husband and raise babies. These were the essential skills. The corollaries: learn to cook just enough and entertain with grace. This was true for Connie and Julita because it was true for me, when my turn arrived. This was the buffet. Pretty ample. Comforting in its consistency. Privileged. But something would be missing for me.

In the rowdiness of that house in Bella Vista, mami's childhood home built by her father, Jicky, you could hear Essie calling, "Jicky come!" to no one in particular. Always she would turn to the telephone and dial her mother, "Mamá, mamá, Freddy is hitting Mikey," and she would put the children on the phone for the certain intervention that would restore the household to a short-lived calm.

When Julita—my mother—had two years of high school left and Connie had four to go, they were enrolled together in a "ladies finishing school," Penn Hall in Chambersburg, Pennsylvania. They both thrived, though mami told us, "I got fat," when she discovered Creamsicles, the painterly orange-and-white ice pops made with vanilla ice cream and icy sorbet. In the middle of the night, Connie would notice feet by her feet and discover her best friend Julita inside her bed, spooked by something and needing comfort.

Mami and tía Connie were married in the same year. Julita, in April, at twenty, and Connie, at eighteen, in November.

After giving birth to Patricia, mami visited a psychiatrist in California.

INSIDE-OUTSIDE

La Misa

One by one, every girl in the queue reaches into the basket by the open double doors and plucks a head covering, a round doily the size of a *yarmulke* pinched with a single bobby pin that does not discredit the sweetness of the tulle and the lace. I attach mine, and I walk in.

We adjust our eyes to the softened light. Opposite the altar, at the foot of the chapel, is a stone bowl half-filled with holy water. Girls who remember dip their middle fingers into the liquid and touch their foreheads to begin the sign of the cross. *En el nombre del padre*, at the forehead, *del hijo*, high on the chest, *del espíritu santo*, left shoulder, then right. Nuns are singing Gregorian chants in the balcony. Voices of angels rain down on our heads. The procession continues down the center aisle. There is a single row of pews on the right and the same on the left. The younger grades settle closest to the metal grille near the altar, the older, high school girls at the back. We genuflect. We slide into each pew from the center axis toward the walls until every pew is filled. Before the priest begins, we kneel onto the wooden ledge that is attached to the seat in front, clutching the petite, shiny white *misales* with white-ribbon tail peering out from gold-edged pages. After the right number of minutes, we sit, and the Mass begins.

Because the prayers are in Latin, the bells serve to alert us that it is time for communion. Voicing rhythmic incantations, the priest lifts the round wafer above his forehead, consecrating it, pronouncing it the body of Christ. The altar boys agitate the bells. Girls who have confessed earlier squeeze past the rest of us in the pew toward the center aisle. They line up quietly in dutiful intention. They approach the priest at the grille and kneel before him.

A girl sticks out her fleshy tongue to receive the gift, the slender, unleavened wafer; then she stands up with lowered eyes. She brings her fingers together and drops her chin to contain the presence that is now inside her and returns to us, walking slowly along a new tributary to the outer end of our pew. The girl steps in, and the rest of us—subdued and empty—slide toward the center to give her space.

I listen for the angel voices. The priest concludes the Mass. "*Ite, Missa est,*" he declares, the Mass is ended. We file out to begin our day.

I long for communion.

Las Esclavas

In any one year there were only three or four of us Jewish girls at Las Esclavas —always *primas*. We were a small group of Jews, about a hundred family units, and those of us *niñas* who attended Las Esclavas had to go to Mass before class like the other girls. The Catholic orders had the only good schools then. Some of my *tíos* chose to send their children to public school in the American Canal Zone with no religious instruction—in spite of the English. Papi wanted us to be *"panameñas primero."* Carlitos attended Javier, run by the Jesuit priests.

When I was in fourth grade, we Jewish girls were allowed to skip Mass, to sit on the pale-green ceramic squares on the steps between floors talking softly and feeling more clashing, unhitched from the seduction of the morning ritual.

After morning classes, we climbed into the bus that took us home for lunch and our siesta in the worst of the heat.

In 1955 two Argentine brothers established the first two grades of the first Jewish school in Panama with the help of our families. It was called Albert Einstein and was open to all religions. (But this happens later.)

Our adviser at school was *madre* Concepción, a massive woman covered completely except for the exposed shield of her face and her hands. She and the other nuns at school wore thick black robes in folds held at the waist by a band and reaching down to the tips of their shoes. I noticed the shoes. What nuns were, I thought I knew, but those squeaky, black leather shoes were radical. Our *mamis* wore pretty, three-inch heels. The nuns sailed down the halls surrounding the courtyard, their dark headdress with a white band across the forehead making their skin very pink. They were a different sort of creature. And they were kind.

Our madres met with parents, but they never left the school grounds. Above their pressed-down chests, they wore a white cotton panel pinned with a carved image of the *sagrado corazón*, the holy heart. They were handmaidens of the Sacred Heart of Jesus. *Esclavas.* Two by two, at any time of day and night, they were in continuous adoration of the *ostia consagrada*, the holy, consecrated wafer exposed in the sanctuary, in the inside chamber defined by the long, bisecting grille of the school chapel.

Judía

Panama, ninety-five percent Catholic, had been a crossroads for trade for hundreds of years, and panameños were accustomed to people of many sorts. But if someone asked, *"¿Eres judía?"* you pulled in a short breath and gulped it down. The word for Jew in Spanish is harsh, the letter "j" sounding like an "h" in English, thrown from the throat across the upper palate. *Hebrea* was a better, softer word, "h" in Spanish having no sound. *Los hebreos* were the people of the book, children of Abraham and Moses, receivers of the Commandments.

"¡Tú mataste a Jesús!" I was sitting in the back of the bus with no way to escape. I still remember the burning words. Eight-year-old Camila had twisted her head to face me. "You killed Jesus!" Small flames circled my spongy heart. The school bus fell silent. We knew the damning fact. We had learned it in *la clase de religión: Judas* the traitor turned in the son of God. *Judas* the betrayer, *un judío.*

The nuns at the school were respectful. We, the Spanish Jews, were an established community, older than the country. Almost *rabiblancos,* the "white-tailed" elite of Panama. Nevertheless I studied *catecismo* and *religión* and learned about Purgatory, where souls with venial sins could take up temporary residence.

"Madre, can Jews go to Purgatory?" I asked.

"Not unless they convert."

"But if you are good and you die before you convert, what happens? *¿Vas al infierno?"*

"*Sí*," replied my teacher. "The rule is that if you have heard of Jesus and don't convert, you cannot be saved."

"What about Limbo? Can Jews go to Limbo?"

"If there was a baby not Catholic who died before he had ever heard the name of Jesus, he can go to Limbo."

Where did I belong? How could these madres who knew my family believe that we would skid down in a giant chute to burn forever with the Devil?

I became a pest at Catechism. Still, the story of Jesus and the tactile wisdom of the tradition were irresistible. There was a glossy rosary bead for each prayer. Our fingers touched the prayer when we recited each sonorous call and riposte.

Patricia and I succumbed. We snuck pink rosary beads into the house and said prayers at night under our bed sheets. When Patricia worried about a boy, she prayed to the Virgin Mary.

"I want to convert," I confessed to madre Concepción. "I want to be a nun like you." The madres held me back for a while, then arranged a meeting with a priest in the front room where they welcomed parents. I poured out my anguish, "*Padre, me quiero convertir. Me quiero convertir.*"

"Niña," he said, "*espere, un poco.* Wait until you're older. You have a fine tradition in your *judaísmo. ¿Sabes?*"

Because I didn't grow up in her time, I never understood the disquiet. At the end of a school day when I might come to visit, my doting Amamá would look up at me with her troubled-blue questioning eyes, "*¿Con quién andas?*" Who are your friends?

She never spelled it out, but I knew that I was meant to unearth an "Arias," a "Vallarino," or another prominent name in Catholic society. I resisted revealing the names of my friends, friends that *did* match what my Amamá longed for. My friends were my friends, Anita, Marce, Ceci, *mis amigas católicas* who lived not too far from *mi casa de piedra* on *calle Uruguay*.

Were Amamá's worries *miedos de un pasado antiguo*? Were they fears of banishment from Spain that coursed in the family blood? Why was mi abuelita so bothered?

Judía Redux

On a Sunday afternoon, tío Stanley and tía Connie are sipping gin and tonics on the patio across the screened door of their living room where Margie and I are twirling to LPs we've stacked on the hi-fi. I always outlast "mi hermanita." I dance my shoes into every corner, blowing against the *sillas y ventanas*. Tio Stanley and tía Connie are looking at me.

Can my tíos live with the slight aberration of me?

I am Jewish, then. Una judía.

Like my cousins, when we cast jacks onto the smooth, tiled floor and toss the red rubber ball in the air. A daughter of my mami, niece of my tios, una de las primas.

I am held by an agreeable pull in the heart of the galaxy.

Not harsh, not inelastic, our family was a closed circle. The grand-child out of wedlock was held, no matter the gossip. The cousin who botched the business, forgiven and rescued. No lighting bolts from the God of the Old Testament. We were probably more Ca-ribbean, easy going. Everyone is entitled to a break.

At the close of Yom Kippur, we gather at tía Connie and tío Stan-ley's house to break the fast. As if we need reminding that we are a clan, all the tíos and primos come together. Even my uncles who married Catholic women and raised their children Catholic come to break the fast.

At tía Connie's white draped table, we reach for the tall silver carafe—hot to the touch—steaming with coffee boiled in cinnamon water. A pretty, distended bowl holds a glossy mound of egg yolks and sugar that have been whipped to a frenzy. We dip a large silver spoon into the white, and we wait while the thick cream drops into our coffee cups with a slow-moving *plop*.

There are not many rules. Ham but not pork. We eat shellfish now. My country is the land of the shrimp. Far from other Jewish groups, we are on our own.

Minyan

Our *sinagoga* Kol Shearith Israel is a long rectangle with stucco walls and a turret in the middle. The sinagoga is on *avenida Cuba con calle Treinta y seis*. There is a *minyan* every Friday night, the required ten men for public worship. The same ten or twelve tíos alternate the roles of *presidente, vicepresidente, o tesorero*. One De Castro, one Fidanque, one Motta or Cardoze or Maduro or Lindo or Toledano—reading at the podium in their *guayaberas*. All tíos. In earlier decades it would have been different men with the same last names, a game of musical chairs. It would have been one or the next and then the same one again sitting on the red leather chairs facing the family in the pews, next to the Ark holding the *Torá* and the Panama flag on its slender pedestal.

An elder reads a prayer for the "Reader" and the group responds with their lines marked "Congregation" or "Chorus" from the blue books stored in slots behind the pew in front. They drone their rumble in English, skipping the prayers in Hebrew except for the *Shema* and the *Kaddish* (naturally using the Spanish inflections, *Cheh-má* and *Kahdeesh*).

I hear the soft thunder of the congregation in the double height above my head. The bells and tiny concave metal discs dance to their own music on the silver finials at the top of the staves holding the scrolls of the Torá.

Las tías organized a school on Saturday mornings at the leftover end of the synagogue. A one-room schoolhouse for primos. It was a long and slender void equipped with square folding tables with tubular legs that kept pieces of your flesh when you clicked them in place. In this shiftable room, the adults also met after Friday night service for a glass of Manishevitz and little chunks of pound cake. We sang from the red hymnal and acted stories from the Bible. I won an award for learning Hebrew words that I did not understand.

Before the Jewish cemetery was consecrated in Panama City in 1876, my ancestors were buried in the Protestant cemetery. During World War I, a chaplain assigned to the Jewish enlisted men in the Canal Zone introduced the tiny clan to the Union Prayer Book used by the Reform congregations in the United States. The group completed a synagogue in 1935 and hired their first rabbi, a young graduate from the Hebrew Union College, aligning themselves with the Reform movement, still clinging to Spanish and Portuguese chants. The rabbi served for five years. There were others, but the community was not able to hold onto a rabbi for long.

There were newer Jewish congregations in Panama: the Orthodox Sephardic community from Syria and other parts of the Middle East who arrived in the 1920s and '30s, and a small congregation made up largely of refugees from Western Europe after World War II.

I imagine that my tíos looked upon the new rabbi's tallit with long tendrils of fringe at the ends and felt connected to an ancient and venerable wisdom. He made them think and called them to moral action. I experienced an occasional visiting rabbi, and that's how I saw it. I didn't have many details.

We were a tiny minority living in a small nation with a capital city set next to the Pacific Ocean, warm and open, an expansive country. We had little reason to complain, and we were careful not to offend.

Apartment 5C

On Friday afternoons I made a point of landing at Amamá's apartment in El Madurito. Then, just before the early pinks of sundown, I took the small elevator to 5C. My aunt's burst of laughter welcomed me as I loitered outside of the door.

"*Quiubo,*" my new best cousin Julieann was happy to sound out her few words of Spanish, "*¡Oye prima, entra!*"

Julieann was more my sister's age than mine, thirteen to my adoring eleven. Her dad—tío Freddy—had moved the family back to Panama after a gap of fourteen years, and Julieann had been born in New York. Julieann was different from my other first cousins. She was dreamy and fun, a little *en las nubes*.

I fixed my eyes on her lashes, curling even more deeply when she rolled on the clumpy mascara, and on her cheeks when she blended little dabs of colorete, smoothing them up to the peak of her cheekbones next to the hairline.

My cousin told me grown-up girl things. Her mother had explained to her "the facts of life," and though the revelations ambushed me at the time, I was more startled by the idea of a mami who could speak to her daughter so plainly.

There was a lot of conversation in 5C, coming mostly from tía Ethel, Julieann's mother, because tío Freddy, the almost-redhead of my mother's brothers, was *muchos amores y abrazos* but a little distant in his focus, not unlike my mami's other brothers. "*Hola mi querida. ¡Te ves linda!*" he would exclaim with foggy abandon.

I worried that mi tía would topple over in her skinny heels. She had a wide middle, and her hips were very narrow. She was always moving, and when she laughed, one of her feet would skip a beat, and she would have to catch herself to readjust the symmetry. It was difficult to unplug your eyes from her. Tía Ethel had a deep curving nose, and her lips were long and fleshy. She would be telling stories, memories of family in crazy predicaments, laughing heartily, pulling us along in her wake. This was done mostly in English or a broken Spanish, for though my mother's brother's wife was a cousin of my father, she had been raised in New York.

I liked her. My American tía made no demands. She wasn't schooled in the measured rules of my other relatives, which distilled to one pure thing, *¡con buenas maneras!* Good manners— and not rocking the boat.

I could slip into this family almost unnoticed.

The furniture that my aunt and uncle had shipped from Long Island was modern. I remember the black-as-oil, kidney-shape coffee table and the linen sheers on the windows with thin colored lines. It was easy to tell, my tíos had good taste. There was a baby grand piano in the corner taking up a quarter of the room. Julieann was good at the piano, and maybe she would be a concert pianist one day.

My tía brought the Friday ritual from New York that no one in our family practiced. Each Friday I headed for the dining room, tiny and square, ready for the moment tío Freddy returned from a day at the store. A silver goblet and two silver candlesticks were at my aunt's place setting with a little box of matches at her knife. On a butler's tray behind the clothed table, there was a braided challah on a plate. My aunt began by lighting each of the two tapers, laughter announcing her hand. She read from the prayer book as she lifted the silver goblet. Julieann's baby sister had a small glass of purple grape juice to sip; the rest of us swallowed from the cup. The challah was unveiled. My aunt sliced it as we recited a Hebrew blessing over bread that I could read in transliteration. Then, she boomed, "Come children!" and Julieann, her sister, and I jumped to her side.

"*May the God of our fathers bless you!*" she said.

"*May He lead you to be an honor to this family.*

"*May He make you a blessing to Israel and all mankind.*"

Pork chops or steak, served with *chayote*, a salad of cut vegetables, and rice would be brought in by the maid. We talked and we ate until just before dessert, when tía Ethel would rise from the table, walk to the piano next to the balcony, and begin to play. We followed along with *ayn kelohainus* and stanzas from "God Is in His Holy Temple." Tío Freddy, who would have pushed his chair back by now, headed toward the piano to stand at her right facing us at the table. We waited for the familiar operatic heights. Tío Freddy was a tenor with a strong voice, which he held in short bursts over the words of his beloved Neapolitan songs.

Non ti scordar di me
la vita mia e legata a te
c'e sempre un nido nel mio cuor per te
non ti scordar di me.

Don't forget me
my life is bound to yours
there will always be a nest in my heart for you
don't forget me.

I did not know that this perfect family would fracture only a few years later, my uncle accepting the invitation extended to men in our Latin American society—a forgiving acceptance of sexual relations with women outside of the marriage. This often meant that the man would have *una querida*—a second wife in practice—and sometimes a second set of children. Wives learned to accept what seemed inevitable.

The worlds traveled by men and their queridas existed in parallel universes that could not be kept apart in the small city of Panama. *Todos sabían.* Everyone knew.

Girls understood what might be in store.

Days of Opera

Every year, when the opera troupe arrived from Italy, my mother's youngest brother—tío Arturo—would beg the impresario to sing to him at his apartment—7C—in the El Madurito. "Lagares, you can't deny us your beautiful voice," tío Arturo would cry out, and water would pool in his eyes, and he would reach for the chair that only he sat on, his chest puffed up in anticipation of feeling.

Of course, el señor Lagares—who was *italo-argentino*—would comply. One knee over the wall-to-wall orange carpet, the impresario would open his arms to an imagined audience and sing a Neapolitan song of love in a rich voice that thrilled us.

"*Es mami con pantalones,*" Patricia and I dared to whisper. Mami with pants. Handsome with long *patillas*, tío Arturo was very vain, effusive with compliments—none of which we believed. "You look *tan bella*"—not missing a beat—followed by "so much better than you looked last week." Still, we yearned for the compliment, and we always got stung.

In advance of the opera troupe, *signor* Frigo—his hair painted red—arrived to train the children's chorus that would participate in the performances. Primos who were musical practiced every morning. Their intricate wardrobes arrived by sea, moldy and damp. La Traviata. Rigoletto. La Bohème. Aida. At el teatro Río or El Cecilia. My tíos sponsored the Italian troupe for three consecutive years and recorded the arias to listen to *todos los dias*—blasting *Quando me'n vo'* or *Si mi chiamano Mimi* on giant JBL and Harman Kardon speakers, brands that they carried in their retail and wholesale business.

I listened from Amamá's open balcony six stories below.

Tío Arturo shared some of the family's neuroses. He talked about his *fobias* and didn't like to be touched, trying to cure his fears by hypnosis *con Pentotal*, searching for doctors in Panama to help with the family's maladies. (With my padrino Walter, he found the doctor who would perform insulin shock therapy—"sugar therapy" they called it—on mami.)

In 1958 mami's brothers sponsored Leonard Bernstein's first

stop of a tour that he and the New York Philharmonic would make through several cities in South America. My uncles selected el teatro Río for the performance, a cinema in an Afro-Antillean neighborhood down river from our still-small capital city. The building had the widest stage and magnificent acoustics. The white panameños would travel that night to Río Abajo for the love of music. It poured that night. There was no changing room and no air conditioning (as was typical then). The musicians' trunks that lined the side of the building were soaked. Performers slipped into their damp dinner jackets in front of passersby.

In other years my tíos sponsored the violinist Joseph Fuchs. Ella Fitzgerald. The San Francisco Ballet. They fashioned themselves as purveyors of the arts in our city, thereby quenching their own thirst for beautiful things.

OCTOBER 3

Did Mami Love You?

I try to imagine papi noticing mami when they were young, feeling a pull toward this pretty cousin—nine years younger than he. So loving to party. So at ease with commotion. "*Mi media naranja*," papi would have admitted. "Half of my orange," a Spanish expression equivalent to "my other half." Without this half, I would not be whole.

When courting her, papi drove mami to Pinotti's for coconut ice cream *hechos en casa* in the old city. They danced to the music of Lucho Azcárraga, a young composer reinventing cumbias on the organ. Julita's complaints about stomach ailments did not alarm Eddie.

I long to ask you, papi. I know that she was fascinating in her wicked need for living. I saw that you loved her and took on her mother's role. Eddie, was this enough?

Eddie, I want to ask you. Did mami love you?

Did mami love me?

Julita was interned at a second psychiatric hospital, the Institute for Living in Connecticut, from 1955 to 1957. My father wrote weekly letters of comfort and encouragement. But mental illness has its own logic, and time was running out.

Letter that papi wrote to mami in August of 1956 when she was interned at the Institute for Living in Connecticut, written in English.

My darling,

If you haven't heard from me in a while it is not because "they haven't been giving you my letters." It's because I haven't written you. Please forgive me, my sweet.

This letter is being written on the typewriter I gave Patricia as a birthday present from you and me. It's an Olivetti portable and is very nice. Since she is studying typing in school she can practice at home.

My darling, we miss you here, and you know it. Neither my life nor the kids' is complete without you. Carlitos is growing up to be a fine boy, although on the short side and is all boy. I am giving him swimming lessons and will make a real swimmer out of him. The girls are sweet and considerate and continue with their guitar.

We all want you back. But you know you are not quite ready yet. To come back the way you left would be wrong for you as well as for us. We are pulling for you and that is what keeps us happy—that this is only a temporary interlude. No my sweet, you are not crazy (this is in answer to your many times repeated questions). But my darling, you have an emotional difficulty that prevents you from seeing that your unhappiness is due to the fact you are unable to accept that your physical ills originate from unconscious thoughts. Believe your psychiatrist who is only trying to help you.

There is not much news since I last wrote to you. I miss you terribly, my love, and sometimes feel at loss with myself. Getting to be a regular old bachelor. At night if I have nothing better to do I go to a movie just for the hell of it. Do a lot of reading.

I feel a little dry today and bereft of news. I'll close now. Keep that chin up.

Love,
Eddie

"Be-Bop-A-Lula"

I first see the nuggets of red curly hair in shadow against the open door. "*Hola, quiubo,*" he calls to me. His eyes are green and peering into mine. Swimming sperm in "*Aquellos ojos verdes.*" It is 1956 and it is rock 'n roll time in the year of innocent stirrings, hormones deployed, not finding a clear destination. Only music and dance—jitterbug around the clock tonight. This was the year of René, my first love. This little girl not even bleeding.

We practiced romance on the backbeat to Bill Haley, Elvis, and Frankie; dance and confessions of love for one sweet year when we were both eleven. Sitting within the veil of the mango tree leaves. A stolen touch on the lips. Light current experiments.

Boleros

The long sliding door between the dining room and terrace had been pulled open for the party. The tías looking on were laughing and unconcerned. Our feet moved in simple box step to the crooning and harmonics of el Trío Los Panchos, the three cupids who plucked the strings of their guitars, egging us on. Some girls were just beginning to bloom, or we were in full flower. We noted the shy hold of some of the boys, and we vibrated to the firm insistence of the practiced ones, a palm pressing hard against our backs, the ears feather linked or clamped together in illicit pleasure. We might signal a halt with a decided pulling back, and then return to the intoxicating embrace. We were chaste and only at the beginning of the love lessons. But the girls, we understood that we were destined for the pure, singular love of "*Solamente una vez.*"

Calypso, mambo, and *cha cha cha* fell on us like a tidal wave from across the Caribbean Sea. The new melodies and the beat filled the lusty spaces of our growing up years. We sashayed to calypso, rocked our hips to "*El negrito del Batey,*" and skipped dripping wet to "*Las clases del cha cha cha.*" For our own traditional *cumbias,* I was taught to glide with gently bended knees under full coquettish skirts, shoulders relaxed, neck open.

Liquid dance and uneven dreams of love held me floating. Floating in space lightly like a *mariposa.*

Engañadora

"Get up, get up, Marlena. There's a fire *arriba. Tenemos que salir. ¡Ya!*"

I had been staying overnight at a cousin's apartment in 6C of the family compound, El Madurito. The fire had started in the room just above where I was sleeping. An American woman had fallen asleep with a cigarette in her mouth.

I was in my baby dolls and felt exposed, so I grabbed a sheet. We ran down the six flights bumping into primos along the way and exited to the front lawn facing the burning floor.

"Only Jicky can save us now," I heard Amamá exclaim. She was on the lawn, but her sister tía Anita was screaming from the balcony at 1A, "Where is Ani? Ani?" Ani was her young grandchild, and tía Anita could not accept that she was safe, already on the grass.

"Jicky come!" continued Amamá, imploring her dead husband to rise from the dead and save us all.

The *monito* Tití, a marmoset, was perched on top of the little girl's head.

Tío Arturo was preoccupied. He had raced down from 7C impeccably dressed, and he paced. He knew that the brothers had no fire insurance on the prized building.

Patricia had slept at Amamá's. In the rush she grabbed the life and death possessions of a teenage girl. With one arm Patricia hugged the rubber *cinturilla* reinforced with long bones that hooked around the middle of our bodies to create a waist. Spilling out of her right arm was a multi-layered crinoline saturated with starch that we called *la engañadora*.

Patricia's Birthday

I was sitting in the dark, enjoying the squeals all around me. Privy to the grand joke.

"*El pobre gato,* poor cat. It was hit by a car just outside of the house."

"*¡Qué tragedia!*"

"Killed right in front of our noses."

Papi and I alternated lines of the story. Each girl as she came into the small playroom was already expecting the worst. Friends of my sister had been corralled in our bedroom next door, and they stepped in one by one into the pitch-black room. They were already in a fever from hearing the screams of their friends.

Each girl was told the sad story of our beloved cat, Gringo. My serious sounding father was convincing.

"We saved some of him. Here, we saved his fur. Feel it."

(This was an old Davy Crocket hat.)

"And his eyes."

(Peeled grapes)

"And his *tripas.*"

(Cooked spaghetti, his guts)

Touching tripas got the wildest shrieks. The hairs on my arms stood straight up at every shrill response. I got scared over again, every time.

It was July thirtieth, Patricia's thirteenth birthday. I was eleven. Carlitos was eight.

October 3

"Patricia," I whispered. "*¿Oíste?*" I leaned into the open space between our beds, into her shadow lifting and then towering above me. I felt a quiver spreading down my back. "*Es Carmen. Esa es Carmen.*"

Why did the maid scream?

Our bedroom windows were fitted with open wooden louvers against steel-mesh screens, and I could hear the heavy rustling of leaves.

"*Vamos* Patricia," I pulled at Patricia. We did put on our slippers, but I didn't think to shake mine that night, to dislodge any tiny creature that might be tucked inside in sweet repose.

We passed our father's books brooding in the dark along the hall. The door to papi's room was open; the air conditioning that offered mild relief was not turned on. Moonlight was peering through the open curtains. The bed was empty.

Sighs again and mumbled words. The light was on at the front, and Amamá was there with Carmen. They were standing by the brick wall just under the painting of the woman who leaned against the turquoise pillow.

"*Papi tuvo un dolor muy malo,*" Amamá said. "He will be okay," she told us. "*No se preocupen.* He went to dinner with tía Glo and tío Donny. He's in the hospital now. *En el San Fernando.*"

Otro ataque del corazón. Was it the heart?

I knew about the first one.

"Niñas," Carmen quieted us. "Niñas, you can sleep in your father's bed tonight. I will call you when it's time for school in the morning."

Carmen asked Amamá, "Who will call la señora Julita in the United States?"

We kissed our Amamá goodnight. And even though the big bed was cool and the faint smell of Aqua Velva aftershave lingered on the pillow, I did not sleep.

It was hard to concentrate that next morning. *Peticote-medias-zapatos-traje-lazito-y-corazón.* I put on the white, heavy cotton dress, short collar buttoned at the neck, and I pinned the small blue tie on top with the metal *sagrado corazón* clasped in the middle.

"Would you go down to Madre Concepción's office?" Madre María Luisa looked at me when one of the novices came up and whispered into her neck. I was in my favorite class, *geografía*, learning names and capitals of African countries that even then were changing.

"Marlena. . . ."

"*¿Yo?*" I giggled and raised my eyebrows to the class. When I left the room with the novice, I passed the open courtyard where another class was doing *gimnasia* in the sun, and two little girls were playing on the slide.

Tía Connie was outside of the nun's office, and she rushed to hug me as I approached. "Manenín," she called out, "I'm taking you home." And in the cocoon of her car, tía Connie told me that doctors had tried many things, but they could not help papi. Tía Connie had come with a chauffeur—which she never used—and sat in the back with her arms wrapped around me the whole length of the way to Urbanización Obarrio. She talked to me through her tears. Tía Connie could never hold back tears.

There were unexpected cars in the driveway and the door to my house was slightly open. I saw first my Amamá, her beautiful face moving toward me and looking very large. Her blue eyes gazed tenderly into my confusion. She said, "He was forty-three. He was such a good man," in English.

There were mostly women at this time of the morning—tías everywhere. The sliding doors to the terrace were fully open. They were standing in relief against the patio that held the calabash tree now empty of *totumas*. Patricia was home. Where was Carlitos?

Patricia told me some years after that when tía Gloria and tía Betty brought her home from school that morning, she tried to go and see papi, "wanting to get to his room and they wouldn't let me . . . feeling that if I had touched him or called to him he would have listened to me and not be dead." I didn't know this about my sister, her wish to fix and be a hero. On that afternoon, as I was wailing in my bed next to hers, and so many people were coming around, she said to me, "I know you're faking it, Marlena."

For weeks and months, when I'd see a man about five foot nine, a little stout, with brown hair and glasses, even if I just saw the hair and the back, my heart would lurch and I would think, *¡Allí esta papi!* I made up a story in my head that papi had gone on a trip for a while and could not tell us why. There was a reason he had to hide. After all, mami was away.

In Neat Palmer Script

Letter I wrote to mami on October 10. Original Spanish. English translation follows.

> *Queridísima mami,*
>
> *Me haces mucha falta y muchísimo más ahora que hemos perdido a mi querido papi que tanto nos adoraba.*
>
> *Tú y nadie más puedes imaginar la falta que nos hace papi.*
>
> *Después que te hablé por teléfono Tío Lionel vino con las cajetitas y son muy bonitas, Muchas gracias. También recibí los mocasines hace un tiempo.*
>
> *Después del entierro vinieron un grupo de niños de mi salón y trajeron una corona para papi pero como llegó*

tarde y él tenia tantas se la pusieron en la tumba de mi
abuelito, el papá de mi papá. Esta tarjetita que está den-
tro de la carta está firmada por la señorita de aritmética
y las niñas que mandaron la corona. Casi todas ellas me
vinieron a visitar.

La niña Mery es buenísima con nosotros especialmente
con Carlitos. Hizo un viaje especial a Taboga para dis-
traerlo, y todo el tiempo nos está haciendo favores.

Amamá, tía Mimí, tía Esther, tía Connie, tía Viviana,
tía Betty, tía Anita y todas las otras tías son buenísimas
con nosotros.

Tía Connie y tía Evi nos mandaron a hacer 2 faldas
para mí y 2 faldas para Patricia y además de eso un vestido
para Patricia.

Me despido con muchísimo cariño

tu hija que te adora
Marlena

My very dear mami,

I miss you and much more now that we have lost my
papi who adored us so much.

You and no one else can imagine how much we miss
papi.

After I spoke to you on the phone, tío Lionel came with
the little boxes and they are very pretty. Thank you. I also
received the moccasins.

After the burial a group of children from my class came
and brought a wreath for papi, but because it arrived late
and he had so many, they put it on the headstone of my
grandfather, the father of my father. The little card that is

inside this letter is signed by the arithmetic teacher and by the girls who sent the wreath. Almost all of them came to visit me.

Our neighbor Mrs. Mery is wonderful with us, especially with Carlitos. She made a special trip to Taboga to distract him, and the whole time she is doing favors for us.

Amamá, tía Mimí, tía Esther, tía Connie, tía Viviana, tía Betty, tía Anita, and all the other tías are wonderful with us.

Tía Connie and tía Evy had two skirts made up for me and two for Patricia and in addition a dress for Patricia.

Goodbye with love

Your daughter who adores you

Marlena

After

Tío Henry, my father's best friend, came to the house to see Patricia. "Tu papi wanted you to have this," he told her. In a pretty box wrapped in yellow ribbon was a pale yellow dress with a wide neck just off the shoulders *y una falda de campana,* the kind of skirt that swooped down in an arc supported by crinolinas. Patricia could wear that color; her skin was olive while I was more pink. She could wear violet too.

"Mariposa," he winked at me. This was tío Henry's nickname for me. When I was little, he told me, I skipped with my arms outstretched and waved them about like a butterfly about to lift off.

In December, three guardians picked for us by papi in his will bought a large turkey for Christmas dinner, and they gathered at our table: tío Henry, tío Lionel, and tío Ralph with their wives; our Amamá, tía Mimí and tía Esther, and our favorite primas. We were fifteen at the table on that Christmas night.

As you wanted, Julita, we bought two playsuits for Marlena, for Carlitos, an erector set. For Patricia a ring with a tiny ruby for her birthday month. The children's presents were placed under the tree with your name, tío Lionel wrote to my mother on January first.

In the wish to shield Carlitos, there began a series of moves to the homes of tíos and friends who had a boy-child his own age. For a year he lived in Honduras with my mother's cousin and his children. He lived for a while in Apt 1C of El Madurito with tío Mikey. La Niña Meri, our neighbor, offered to adopt him. Amamá moved her head from side to side. "Julita will need her son!" And that was that.

Cousins to my parents in New York, who'd been papi's eyes and ears when mami arrived at the Institute for Living, invited Patricia to stay with them in March. "Patricia as the eldest should visit Julita. It'll do them both good."

My sister wrote from New York, *I saw Batista's daughter. (He's the president of Cuba!) She's in the hospital too. And Gene Tierney, the beautiful actress. She plays bridge with mami.*

We don't have the medical records of mami's stay at the Institute. Gene Tierney's biographer describes an era of shock treatment for the actress who was suffering then from a severe depression. Gene Tierney interned herself at the Menninger Clinic years after her stay at the Institute for Living. My mother would follow this pattern many years later.

Mami returned from The Institute for Living in Connecticut in June. "I don't have a husband," she wailed.

Our mami was still mami.

*

In that year that papi died, I got my eyeglasses. *Tenía miopía*, like papi. I didn't mind the new appliance that sat on my face with brown rims that matched my hair. From my side of the glass, I could see a space that spilled out on the edges, an oblique new place that only I knew about.

A giant pine tree was missing from our yard. I hugged the missing tight until I couldn't find it.

OTHER GALAXIES

The Gods

The Canal Zone was a little fragment of heaven. From avenida Cuatro de Julio, one of the poorest quarters in Panama City with decaying wood framed buildings, panameños looked across the road in wonder. Great mowed lawns surrounded two- and three-story buildings white as chalk. Some buildings sat regally on stepped pedestals. Others stretched with the landscape to accommodate the sensible labor of invisible workers. Chunks of jungle were manicured to perfection.

The infallible white, the mostly red hipped roofs, the insistent green. This likeness was stamped again and again in the civilian towns and military bases in the American zone. Few panameños came in contact with the people who lived in this measured paradise. We saw the ones whose job was to keep us out. The military police who checked credentials, tall and fit in their sharply pressed uniforms.

The Canal Zone was ten miles wide—five miles on either side of the Canal—and it cut fifty miles across the narrow waist of Panama like a cinch belt separating one part of the nation from another. When we traveled from Panama City to the other provinces, we had to drive across this piece of real estate leased "in perpetuity" by the United States in 1904.

The engineering and medical conquests that made the Canal possible were distant legend to me. American engineers, a military administration, and laborers—the white men paid in gold, black men from the Caribbean paid in silver—cut a canal through mountains, rerouted waterways, engineered locks to lower ships to ocean level. Dr. Gorgas, Chief Medical Officer, eradicated yellow fever and malaria. It took ten years to link the two oceans.

We drove into the Zone up to the big metal swing bridge where we had to wait for the clunky halves to pull apart to let a cargo ship cross the waterway before we could proceed further through the American zone and land in sleepy Panama again to continue on our journey.

Mami, widowed at thirty-four, found herself a new man, a civilian engineer in the American zone. They met while playing bridge and drinking at the Officer's Club in Curundu, a military base. Very-handsome Bob. Four-times-divorced Bob. Tall with an aquiline nose and gentle nature. How did mami land *ese mango*? They married against all *consejos*. I was thirteen.

I acquired a six-year-old sister—a postscript to Patricia who had been sent to a boarding school just before mami remarried. I moved to the other side of Cuatro de Julio, into a concrete duplex with a carport underneath and glass-louvered windows—a matching home to all the other homes on the hill at Fort Kobbe. This time I could get past the guardhouse.

Tasteless canned string beans, *Tang,* and topless children on tricycles racing down the hill. Screaming mothers calling the dinner bell. Paper-thin walls conducting sounds, a creaking bed, parents' grunts and wails.

There is a sweet honeymoon phase when I have a friend, manly and kind. Hard-drinking Bob was an algebra teacher once, and he helps me with my schoolwork. "You are an intelligent girl," he says, "so unlike the rest of your family that I'm sure you take after your dad."

My six-year-old roommate, Sis, with straight yellow bangs, stares into the mirror talking to her secret self in English. She jumps on mami's furniture. There are terrible fights.

"Your daughter, Sis. . . ."

"What's more important, a child or a chair? What's more important, Julita!"

Mami full of questions, incessant questions at the dinner table every night. "When did you go to lunch, Bob? Sandy saw you in Curundu at three. What were you doing there? In Curundu? I know you are lying to me, Bob. You are a liar. You are a liar. . . ."

There were different topics and the same topic every night. Carlitos and I listened, ready to jump at our mami, pulled in sympathy toward our stepfather, knowing exquisitely well why he might want to punch her. We watched in horror as Bob grabbed mami by the throat in a frantic moment. We appreciated the dilemma. We could hardly stand it. The questions—we had always suffered the questions.

Spanish Tears

I get on the bus at the top of the big hill to attend my new American high school. How frightened I feel. This is so different from my all-girls' Catholic school. There are boys on the bus showing off. I hold my eyes to my lap. We land at the start of the colonnade leading into Balboa High School. *¿Dónde voy?* Everyone seems to know, except me. I hold my breath to stop the tears and slip into a building, nearly unconscious, not seeing a rusty nail that rips the flesh off my foot. Now I can release the flood of Spanish tears.

I discover the pleasures of boys pulling my hair from behind, of kind and beautiful Mr. Case, the math teacher. I change discreetly in gym class one layer held over the layer coming off, always veiled like a Muslim woman in full chador. In Homeroom I learn to bake pineapple upside-down cake. I make a friend, pretty, blonde Diane, and I visit her at Albrook Air Force Base. I begin to move into English, to feel some comfort in that difficult tongue, although I know that I am an alien, a "panamaniac," as Kenny in the bus reminds me.

Mi prima Margie comes to stay at Kobbe from time to time, and we loiter in the yard next to the carport where the maid hangs the wet laundry. When walking by the barracks, we smile shyly when we come upon a soldier. We feel comforted by the presence of these orderly Americans who seem to know how to conduct their business. We try not to breathe when the DDT trucks roar by our side. It is 1958. We stroll by the lawns in Balboa, the civilian administrative center, a tropical Hollywood back lot maintained almost imperceptibly by Big Brother. We are strangers in a strange land, safe because we have family. And we can cross the road and be home.

The Canal Zone vanished almost instantly on December 31, 1999, by agreement between the two nations. Rows of identical buildings still exist, some painted by Panamanian owners in brilliant colors, disordered as life.

Robertito is conceived in my year in the Canal Zone. This is a lasting gift from mami. A new brother for me.

Braniff Flight

Amamá and tía Anita drove with us to Tocumen, the single-room Tocumen airport of 1960 with a flat roof where we watched airplanes arrive and waved at friends who were departing. There was no coolant of any sort. We were unmistakably close to the Equator, the air a tepid weight on my skin and clothes—a barricade of heat.

There was one small *botica*, and of course there were *"holas"* for the ladies that Amamá knew when she stopped at the tiny drugstore to buy some Dramamine, in case I got queasy during the flight. Carlitos was there and Margie. I don't see Patricia by my side. She may have been leaving for school later that summer, as mami and I were headed for the United States early so she could buy me clothes for winter at Peck & Peck in New York.

At the airport everyone was teary. But not me. I was pitch-perfect ready for this enterprise. My brow was smooth, and I could see forever. I was going to *los Estados Unidos de América,* to the snow, to the streets paved with gold and lined with Cadillacs, on my first airplane ride. On my first real adventure.

Many months earlier, as I was turning fifteen in late March just after my new brother was born, los tíos—Henry and Ralph and Stanley—had conferred, and they approached my mother, telling her that it was time for me to join Patricia at school. The family knew about the fights in Kobbe and the disintegrating marriage. Patricia was already at the school, in what I discovered later was a stinky paper-mill town in Pennsylvania, up a long and steep hill where the girls' boarding school also kept stables of horses. I was to join other sophomores in an oddly blessed place stranded in the heart of the Appalachian Highlands.

The idea of boarding school *en los Estados Unidos* was not shocking. Mami had done it with her best friend, Connie, two years at Penn Hall in Chambersburg, Pennsylvania. My great uncle had been sent to England generations before, to fan off his wild antics. There was a fluency with this concept in my family. After all, my ancestors had been travelers, sometimes against their will. We had lived in Spain and Portugal, England, Holland, Jamaica, St. Thomas, and other islands in the Caribbean. There was family in New York and in France.

Amamá followed mami and me to the rickety metal staircase outside leading to the plane. She angled her head; she had a folded bill between her fingers—five dollars—neat. "You don't have to spend much," she said as she gave it to me. To mami she said, "Julita. Don't worry so much, Julita."

Nueva York

There was no gold on the streets. The city looked dirty and old. Not the red-tiled roofs and the white cement apartments with balconies of my city. Not the unrelenting vegetation that made corrugated-metal-roof structures look festive in the countryside. *Nueva York* was brown. Worn buildings next to new, very tall ones. A jumble, *un enredo*.

Peck & Peck vocabulary: car coat, lamb's wool gloves, plaid and corduroy, Shetland sweater, pleated skirt, knee socks, ear muffs, and muffler.

Boys' Raid

I was assigned a roommate at the school. Sally was from Pennsylvania. We had suite mates across the bathroom that included a girl from Buenos Aires. Sally, we learned, was promiscuous, although other than at an occasional forlorn "mixer" we never saw boys at the school. Instead, we listened to Frank Sinatra's *Only the Lonely* in an almost continuous loop.

I liked Sally because she was who she was and not afraid to do the wrong thing. There was a queer power to this in a girl's school. Sally had a friend who fawned on her whom she repaid by bossing around or—worse—by ignoring. I watched this for months until my temper ignited, and I lectured this girl in a boiling Spanglish. *"¡No seas una víctima!"* My body was quaking. I heard myself say, "Whining won't work. It won't work," though it had worked for mami.

Sally was thick and not especially tall, but she had beautiful breasts with deep aureolas. Though Sally may have had problems at home, she never talked about them. She recognized her treasure. Used it to get something she needed.

One middle of the night in the middle of the term, I woke up to a boy's face next to my face. He was bent on his knees at the edge of my bed. He whispered my name. His fingers brushed my shoulder; the tips reached my breast. I whimpered. I saw a double silhouette in the dark. Sally, I could tell, was engaged in heavy kissing.

"Leave my roommate alone!" she commanded. The boy withdrew his hand and pulled away.

The invasion by the small band of boys was quickly discovered. They escaped through the kitchen exit in the basement, the secret exit that Sally pressed into service in the dark of night. Sally was expelled just days before the end of the school year. Her grim-faced father came to fetch her. I knew something would not be right for Sally. I admired Sally's daring. I was docile then.

New

Knit purl, knit purl: I made a long striped scarf for myself, a meandering snake of wool, red and black.

Field hockey junior varsity: selected first line of defense swinging that "l-shaped" stick and trying not to get it in the shins.

Tennis: a first, to counteract the primordial *gimnasia* patterns on the patio at Las Esclavas and nights of dancing to Lucho Azcárraga in my city.

Stunt Night: still a fancy for dancing. On this evening, the highland fling of *Brigadoon*.

Giving haircuts: a certain flair that could always be improved by continuous matching of one side to another until the medium length tresses surrendered their predilection.

Mess hall vocabulary: sloppy joes, shepherd's pie, sauerkraut, and flaming baked Alaska. Like mami in her time, I put on weight.

Geometry: postulates and theorems, isosceles and scalene, hypotenuse and radius. Geometry transported me to a peaceful dimension of the mind. I was a maize-colored sponge, the kind that you buy flattened. To fill up was enough.

Biology: On furlough from classification lists in *botánica* and *zoología* at Las Esclavas, I began learning about the human body and also the frog's. The teacher was male; he was not *un mango*, but there we were in the desert. Mr. Blank was so correct and definite and, well, a man. At the dinner table one evening Mr. Blank said, "There are women who dress for women and women who dress for men." I asked for clarification, and he said, "Marlena. You dress for men."

I did cinch my belts, and I wore my shirtdresses tight.

Patricia was a senior. She was dreaming in that complicated year and getting tons of demerits (another vocabulary word) for skipping required activities. She and I spoke in Spanish, and sometimes I hung out with her *latinoamericana* friends, a new label for me too, in the big EEUU (which is how we abbreviate Estados Unidos in Spanish). As Patricia's little sister, I could wish myself invisible when the older girls with quivering Spanish accents read passages from *Lady Chatterley's Lover*. I could shadow them into the bunker for seniors below ground where they puffed on cigarettes trying to whisper double rings into the murky air.

Everyone was a curious specimen to me. We had been plucked and placed in this school that seemed to have no trace of class. All the girls were white, and almost all were Protestant. I might after all not burn forever because I was not *católica*. The proof was with all these Protestants. The whole world could not be going to the deep, hot place that I was destined for.

My friend Linda was waif-like with very fair skin, her hair color almost the same as her complexion, a kind of yellowy-green, very light brown, pin straight and held back with an ordinary rubber band. Linda's dresses were colorless and thin. In winter she wore a simple sweater or a basic coat. Linda spoke softly, and I could tell that she was smart.

Since my home was far away in Panama, I behaved like a candidate for president, traveling from place to place, getting to know the people. During a school break, I accompanied Linda to her home in Alexandria, Virginia. Linda's house was on a flat piece of land with some scrub grass, mostly dirt, straight-up siding, and very little detail. I discovered that her brother, who was older, had built the house in the back of the property when he married. The food was pleasant and the family was nice. Like Linda, they did not make much of a fuss. Their voices were measured as they spoke about John Kennedy, the new American president, unlike my relatives who showed their feelings with animated hands, quick to warn us about any missed cue of manners. Linda had gotten a scholarship to our school. She was wry and funny in her quiet, transparent way. Maybe we were both outsiders and recognized this.

Snow

Lee pointed at the window during English. There was a light white dusting outside. "It's snowing!" she screamed, and the class ignited. The teacher turned to me with mischief on her face. Then she wiggled her eyebrows in the direction of the door; I understood. I got up and walked out into the hall, pushed on the heavy door to the outside, and there it was. Almost nothing.

I stuck out my tongue and felt a few cold pinpricks, but I couldn't see the crystal shapes that we had studied. My heart was pounding in anticipation of something. By sundown snow had begun to accumulate, and the girls taught me how to make angels in the snow. I spent hours and hours making angels until dark, hair stringy, my fingers, rocks.

The next morning, the snow resisted my progress and crawled into my boots.

*

Cold vocabulary: evergreen, army blankets, sleet, sludge, sled, ice skates, snowballs, glistening, blustering, bitter, hail, blizzard, qué frío!

Mami's letter of November 6, 1960, my first year in the US, original in longhand, written in English. My father's brother Monty who lived in Aruba has died, like papi also very young.

My dearest Patsy and Marlena,

It's been a long time since I've written you, maybe when I've been home I've been busy cleaning, etc, as I haven't had a cook.

I don't know if you heard of the terribly sad news about tío Monty, he passed away from another heart attack about a week ago. I hope you've heard the news already as I hate to be the first to tell it to you. I feel so sorry for poor tía Lilla and the children. He was everything to them. Such is life. Tía Mimí and tía Esther went to Aruba right away.

Well now I'm going to try to answer all your questions. I received both of your letters. Patsy I'm sorry to have to tell you this but tío Henry says there isn't enough money to send you to Europe after your graduation. Please tell Mrs. Dunnhill and thank her for her letters. Why don't you write Amamá and see if she can do it? I doubt it, as it's a lot of money. If I had it I'd let you go, but you know I haven't. I would have loved you to have gone away on that trip, it would have been most interesting. I haven't included your monthly money as haven't been paid as yet for the house. As soon as I get it will mail it to you.

Marlena I was very pleased and happy with your report card and that your deportment was good, that's how it should be. Maybe next month you'll be in the A honor roll, as Bob and I figure that this month you had a B average. Bob feels that you'll soon get in the A average. I showed your report card to tío Henry and he was very pleased. I'm glad that you like Roberto's pictures. I'm enclosing a colored one. When you tell him "pan pan" he starts spanking himself. He's too cute. Take the $22.50 for the round trip to Washington from your bank account, also about $30 to buy your evening dress. Will tell tío Stanley this so that he knows how you spent the money. Try to get yourself a red one as you look beautiful in <u>red</u>. Get some <u>chapstick</u> for the dryness of your hands and lips. For the third of November Panama was very quiet. I stayed home the whole day as <u>don't have a cook</u> and I have the nurse off that day. At night I got a fourteen-year-old baby sitter and went to play bridge at the club.

Well my dearest little girls will stop now, and will write you another letter in a few days.

Julita

Girls in Pastel

We wore pink, blue, yellow, turquoise, and pale green cotton dresses in the late summer at the start of school and in the spring when we danced around the Maypole. On a switchover date, we'd turn the page on the calendar firmly, the girls sobering up with mix and match selections for fall and winter: straight, A-line, or pleated skirts. Black, navy, or gray.

Margie and I learned to wash the bathtub rings of soapy grunge. On our white school shirts, we knew to let a heavy iron sit on the cotton collar until the steam billowed up, like our *lavanderas* at home, the women from the Caribbean Islands who had gumption to work from house to house in our city.

After Patricia graduated from our school in Pennsylvania, I had joined Margie and her sister Gay at Dana Hall, a girl's "prep school," set in a pretty New England town near Boston, shortlisted with other elite schools alongside Exeter and Andover academies for boys. We slept in converted Colonial houses under the watchful eye of a "housemother." We took our classes in the rambling Main Building that had a stately, wood-paneled living room where we gathered after meals. The school had been established by Protestant reformers, and most of the girls were Protestant. There was a small mix of Catholic and Jewish girls and foreign girls.

Rebecca had been pre-matched for me before I arrived: a new roommate at my new American school. We were both Jewish, and we were both short, though I didn't know I was short until I looked level at her during our daily walks to class.

Rebecca was fiery and didn't smile much. I can almost imagine seeing lines on her face, not on soft pink cheeks but on flat, tawny skin. She had very dark hair longer than mine and dark brown eyes darker than mine, but when I looked at her I forgot I was another. Feeling my mind but looking at her. We might have been twins. Rebecca was misplaced in some way, and coiled tight. I see her face and her person—not mine—and I feel small and forlorn and separate from the others.

You should see my roommate," one of the girls whispers fiercely to another. "She holds down the back of her tongue to regurgitate her food." I watch the tall girls in pastel who seem to hold together like a clump. Do they know what they are doing? Are they peering out from a narrow window? Faking it like me?

Margie's beauty and grace enact their magic again. Her confidence and sweetness fan out like a beautiful dress. The short and thick blond hair lends her the air of a princess. We have only just arrived, and the sophomores make her president of their class. I am a year older, hiding behind mi hermanita's pastel skirt, sitting in the dim corner of her tiny dorm room watching her friends from a great distance that I cannot negotiate.

I began a letter to tío Stanley in my pretty Palmer longhand:

> *It may sound strange of me writing this to you, tío Stanley. But I'm really lost. I'm on my own with wonderful opportunities, taking some but rejecting those for which I would have to give up something of myself. When something seems too tough, or just a little tough, I escape into a dream world, and then I can't concentrate for days.*

Latinoamericana

Gloria was short and chatty with a huge elegant nose like the American Indian Geronimo. She was a romantic, effusive, and that froth of sounds and feelings noticing every plus and minus in her life was comforting. Gloria lived in Barranquilla, a coastal city in Colombia, one hour's flight from my city. Gloria despaired about her boyfriend.

I opened one of his letters—to help her (I said to myself). When she discovered my transgression, Gloria pretended to be mad. *"¡Te mereces un buen jalón de orejas!"* she screamed. "Tell Margie to pull on your ears for me! *Marlenita, tú me dices que Gabriel me quiere. Yo no creo eso. No se por qué al leer sus cartas lo odio, lo odié, y no veo sino mentiras y mentiras. ¡No! Yo no lo puedo ni quiero querer.*" The abridged American version of a Colombian girl's misery: "He's a liar, Marlenita. I hate him."

In November Gloria announced, inviting me to Barranquilla for the Christmas break, "*Marlenita, Marlenita, me daría tanta alegría si me acompañaras. Mis padres y amigos te van a adorar.*"

When we arrived in late December, Gloria's parents welcomed me with *besos* on both cheeks in the South American way. Their house was a two-story structure that had a wide porch with a balustrade in the front and an enormous wooden stairway to the second floor, ancient and very Spanish, unlike the newer, apartment-living in my city. My country had grown differently from other Latin American nations; its economic life was not dependent on agriculture or mining. Panama was a transit artery. Geography and commerce defined it.

When I joined Gloria's family for dinner that evening, I saw the longest, darkest, carved wood table in an equally gigantic room. Gloria's father sat at one narrow end and her mother at the other. You could not see both without twisting your neck from one shoulder to the other. The butler and the maid attended to us solemnly.

We danced every night at chaperoned parties. "*El Negro*" looked at me. He was formal: *un colombiano* from the capital city. Beautiful, darker than his brothers. Gloria and I partied until two. The next day we'd spring open our eyelashes in the afternoon like princesses in a palace. She had a buzzer in the bedroom that she pressed with one finger for the maid who would arrive in the time that it took to climb the stairs, neat in a white uniform, carrying a tray with our *cafe con crema y azúcar, fruta y panecillos*. While the "excess" in Barranquilla seemed extreme to me, it was only different from my life in a matter of degree. I too was privileged by class and by the color of my skin.

The latinoamericanas seemed to be more feeling, more suffused with family as I knew it. We looked into each other's eyes. We called out, "*Quiubo, que tal, mucho gusto,*" but we were entrenched in a culture that was set, the classes were set, the expectations.

> *Tío Stanley, I hate to be fake and most of the times I have to be fake in dealing with people. It's not that I don't want to have friends. I think I do because I feel very lonely many times. But, although these girls must and I know have a lot in common with me, I can't get through a kind of barrier that I put up or somebody puts up. Am I strange? Is it wrong to like to be alone most of the time? I love to walk by myself (especially now since Spring is nearly here!) sometimes I feel empty and lonely because I have some ideas (many ideas) I'd like to discuss with someone else. I'd like to hear interesting ideas from other girls. My roommate isn't usually interested in the same things I am, and of the other girls I know quite well they don't seem to be interested either, or they are too busy thinking about other things. I'd like to talk with teachers but they are too busy too. Margie is about the only person (of which I know) who is really interested in the things I am, in the world, in the last thing we studied in our last class. She's the only person that I know is interested! Alive! Of course there must be*

many more people, but I just haven't met them or haven't tried to get to know them.

I just wanted to ask someone, maybe you tío Stanley or tía Connie might know of some answer.

THE PUZZLE OF THE WORLD

Centro del Mundo

I had a secret crush on Miss Fisher. Miss Fisher was so smart, and lean, and logical. Her hair was cropped tight on her sculpted face, her skin scrubbed and shiny. No red on her lips. No lines on her lids. I studied her intently. But today Miss Fisher was facing the class with a poisoned arrow aimed at my heart. "I took Panama!" she declared quoting Teddy Roosevelt, pointing her finger at me.

I am blank on what happened next. The blood drained from my head. Or the arrow pricked my lung instead and stole the air from it.

We were taught in Las Esclavas to revere the framers of our independence in 1903 from Colombia. Belisario Porras—Marcelita's grandfather—was one of our heroes. I had learned that Panamanian liberals fought for autonomy of the province for years. That the United States had plotted with Colombia against them, until the americanos had a change of heart. Teddy—the myopic man on horseback—would be poised to build a canal—something that the French had failed to do—when Panama became independent.

In 1903 the USS *Nashville* visited the coast of Panama, discouraging Colombia from a fight with the feisty province.

My tiny land, its arms grabbing at the north and south hemispheres in the Americas, was center of the world. I had been taught to recite this in grade school: "*Panamá, centro del mundo, corazón del universo.*" Panama, heart of the universe, its arteries fed by thunderous rains.

The puzzle of the world had shifted.

In this school I read my first American works: *Our Town, The Scarlet Letter, Little Women, Uncle Tom's Cabin, To Kill a Mockingbird, Huckleberry Finn, Catcher in the Rye, Of Mice and Men.* The story of the colossus in the north was creeping stealthily into my consciousness. In Massachusetts I began a slow acculturation to an American world that was still a mystery. I was a panameña who understood a little but missed much of the culture that I was slowly embracing.

Buffalo

I don't remember much about Buffalo. I remember it was cold. Very white. Nothing much to notice but the white. Crunchy, desolate white. Wood-framed houses. Could I have traveled there during winter break in my senior year? Or was it in March and there were still mounds of snow? Rebecca's parents looked old to me. They didn't fix themselves up like my family did. Rebecca asked her parents if she could visit me in Panama and had a shouting match that I could hear, her parents making no attempt to muffle the words: "Don't trust your friends, Rebecca. Friends will betray you. In the end it's only family that counts." Rebecca won that fight because she did visit me in the summer. Mami made a place for us in the small extra room that had the TV and flat, bed-like sofas making an "L" in a corner with pillow rolls at the back. Mami loved to feed Rebecca rice with *porotos and plátanos endulzados* and watch her eat, offering her more *de todo,* not worried about her weight.

In my senior year I signed up for a groundbreaking Far Eastern History class taught by Dr. John Schuler, a huge man with a booming voice who traveled a decade later as adviser to Richard Nixon in the People's Republic of China. Dr. Schuler printed a syllabus (new vocabulary word), a long list of books and articles that we should be reading, not pages from a text. There probably were no school texts about China then.

A person's primary obligations in China were to family, he said, and narrated the often-told story: the eldest son in a family plays on the floor with the rattles and stuffed animals of an infant to make his aged parents feel young and happy again. In the United States—we knew—personal independence was primary. Dr. Schuler asked us to build mobiles to show the balance of powerful forces within China, to role-play magistrate, scholar, Ching official. I didn't unfold the syllabus. I didn't understand much. Years later—still holding the images in my head—I would be ready to learn. The Chinese, too, believed that they were the pulsating heart of the world. And the Americans.

I was beginning to cherish the multiple perspectives that came naturally to me. I had been a minority in Panama and could always see the other side.

Lately we have had gorgeous weather. It's pretty cool but sunny and blue, blue skies.

Will have to do a little work for two term papers this va-cation. Will also read a couple of books. Margie got elected a member of council for next year.

I dosed with No-Doze before a test or paper. Joined bull sessions before an exam. Curiosity pulled me through in spite of my now bulging sadness. When I called Amamá and told her I wanted to go to college, Amamá said, "Why, Marlena? Why do you need college? Come home. Work as a secretary. Then you'll get married and have children."

Paper Dolls

I don't want to be a paper doll girl. They come ready-made with smiley faces; maybe one is drawn with a pout. The camera in my head pulls back sharply, back and back. The paper doll girls are flat and flat. Their crinolined dresses are held with white tabs that cinch the waist. The scooped and armless tops circle around the bust.

The voices of the paper doll girls are moving fast in the air.

"*Esas cholitas* can't use a washing machine."

"They take the hand-held *rayador*, and they scrub and scrub and destroy."

"Mine is pregnant. Big as a house."

"*No saben cuidarse.*"

The paper doll girl bites into the deviled egg passed by the maid dressed in pink pastel. Other servants hang back in the cool heart of the house away from the heat, their own cameras flashing discreetly.

Cars beep and beep outside of the open, screened windows. Where's the girl who's engaged?

"Antonio, my hairdresser. *No sé que pasó.* He ruined my hair."

The paper doll girl brings the tips of her fingers to her hair. She puffs up the tease. The camera notices a stain just beginning. Paper doll girls perspire.

The paper doll girls lift their fingers and touch their hair.

They swish their skirts.

They hold an *empanada* neatly and bite with the edge of their teeth.

They look at each other in admiration

A MOTHER LIKE YOU

Julita, You Have to Get Out!

Robertito was eleven months when mami left the duplex in Fort Kobbe, when she packed her baby and belongings and the black Noguchi table.

The MPs had been summoned to the duplex, to bruises on mami's arms. Another time it was a broken ankle. The marriage to Bob had imploded.

"Julita, you have to get out!"

Cousins offered mami a house next to Connie until she could find an apartment near Amamá. Mami accepted, bewildered and numb. She would move to her city, to family, to old routines, demoted—*otra vez*—to a single life. In frantic pursuit of the forfeited one.

I want to be delicate, but I think you will understand, Bob wrote to me at school trying to make sense of his life. *It was emotional attraction. I hope you will forgive me, if I speak plainly, Marlena. It's a horrible thing to be married and find that the things that you have in common are only "emotion." In other words, honey, you can't spend your life in bed!*

Amamá called me long distance at school. "Has mami written to you about Bob? Tell me, why does she love him?"

Patricia was home from her senior year in high school and was enlisted as chauffeur, helping to search for the errant husband, though by now mami was divorced. Mi hermana was caught inside of mami's story, in mami's soliloquy of wrongs and suspicions, privy to the old lovers' trysts.

I was still in school in Massachusetts. Carlitos was living with tío Henry and his wife, Adelaide.

Mami's Harmless

"I know she's there," mami growls sotto voce. Her thumb flies up to the bottom of her upper teeth, pressing up, pressing. I am home on vacation on her side of this call and I know what's coming by heart. Mami takes a sip of water and looks vaguely in my direction. "He's a liar," she mumbles to herself, then returns to the mouthpiece, "Little Stanley, I know Connie's right next to you, *mentiroso.*"

"No, tía Julita, no. . . ."

Stanley my little cousin is six. He's fair, very fair; his teeth are still crooked and brown because he was a preemie. He loves tía Julita. His heart's in a clutch, but he thinks my mami's harmless, another color in the rainbow of family. Even at his age, he can notice that she's sexy and that every year mami drives the latest model Ford that she gets wholesale from my uncles.

Tía Connie, at last, rescues her son and holds the heavy black receiver to her ear. "Here I am," she tells my mother in a weary voice.

"I knew you were hiding from me, Connie. I know that Paulina had a party. I'm a witch. You and everyone else were invited except me. Because you have a husband!" Mami drops the earpiece on its cradle with a raggedy crash, pushes her thumb up against her teeth for another lost minute, then gets up and walks away.

Everyone in the family sucks up a little of mami's craziness. They've all agreed to share it without formal pact. They love her even. I want to scream at mami that she's irritating people. How can they love me when I have a mother like you?

Mami's portrait painted in full color.
It hangs today in Roberto's house.

I was home in the summers. I had gained twenty pounds—my belly and thighs were inflated and puckered—and encountered a mother who insisted on living as I was shutting down in disgust at myself. Mami exercised every morning and pestered Patricia and me to join in. Of course we did not. She labored so hard to maintain the illusion of glamour, her daughters missing some bewitching ingredient that she believed was essential. The culture around us was resolute in its limited view of women and girls. Patricia and I were a measure of her, and we didn't add up.

"I don't want people to forget I'm alive," she cries out, as she clasps pearls to her neckline and wrists. In the mornings mami visits the family store, *saludando* the salesgirls with vigor while trying yet another skin lotion that will dependably leave its greasy, pink residue on her clothes. She smokes with abandon. The crest of ashes holds on to a fading memory, then relents. The salesgirl's anxious fingers push an ashtray under toppling cinders and catch them before I can exhale.

Tun, tun, tun, the girl knocks softly. "*Por favor, señora Julita. . . .*" The next-door neighbor has sent her maid to complain. Mami's been blasting her records again. Judy Garland pours out her heart, drowning out my mother's anxiety and spiking up mine.

"*Mierda*," mami whispers in her throaty way. She turns the dial on the hi-fi a fraction of a millimeter, walks to her bedroom, and closes the door, switched already to a different thought.

Carlitos, still climbing trees to reach for *jobos* and *mamones*, serves as chaperone for mami at the amateur Theater Guild in the Zone, mami arriving late and snoring loudly midway through the production.

"*¿Quién te diseñó el pelo? ¡Se te ve lindo!*" A compliment to a friend about her hair is followed by the irresistible, "It looked terrible before." Mami plays her childlike honesty well. If she is crazy, she is free to speak her mind. It makes people laugh in secret admiration.

In Panama gracious social dealings trumped plain speaking. Mami exploded this notion by exhibiting her dazzling smile while she served a reckless truth. When she wanted her brothers to help with the rent—"After all, I don't have a man,"—she would add, "*Ese hermano es una mierda, un carajo de mierda, pero lo digo con amor.*" "That brother is a s**t, but I say this with love."

¡Nada!

"*Te vez horrible,*" she told us. "You look terrible," and, I have to admit, sometimes with a smile, "*Te ves linda,*" and we lived with her monstrous anxiety on top of our own. When she loaded her body with jewels, I swore that this was not me. When she painted her face, she looked like a witch—which she was—staring into the mirror for hours, crushed cigarettes in the ashtray next to the clogged makeup sponges, the eyes communicating with some story inside the mirror that I wanted to run from.

I didn't want to be me, and I didn't want to be her. Not her. Not the language of compliments of my people, false communications, it was all nada. Nothing to do with what I was or I wasn't. I angled my vision away from that version of family and turned it toward my more serious tíos with clear-headed thoughts. I would watch and think and never be false. Little pearl earrings. No bows. And true. And sad. I was not going to be like her. Not at all.

Bridge

Mami prepared her two tables for afternoon "bridge desserts" with precision. A small ashtray set down at the corners exactly, with a miniature box of matches on top. She served Coca-Cola with a bucket of ice close at hand to replenish the clear cubes that surrendered so quickly in the tropical heat. "Thank God for bridge!" Amamá would exclaim. Mami was an ace, though she talked constantly while she played, seeking every detail in the social life of her friends.

Papi had often said, "Julita, you have such a talent for people." This was true. Mami had made friends in the Canal Zone, very attractive women whose husbands were too busy or distracted. Mami introduced them to the rhythms on the sweet side of Panama. She offered them a taste of the country where few Zonians ventured and contact with a cultured community, easy going and worldly. They loved her parties and lunches at the Club Unión where they'd end up "*en la cantina*"—as mami would say—drinking with upper class, rabiblanco, married men. They loved the bridge games, weekends at the beach. Some became "family," bearing with grace mami's torment. Others, being at some remove, enjoyed her readiness for celebration in spite of the anxiety that shadowed her.

In the 1970s, mami won a huge bridge tournament on a cruise ship that was crossing the canal—over one hundred tables—playing with a partner that she had never met. The reigning Panama champ was livid!

One Summer Night

"Did you miss me? I really missed you," he said, with that smile in his eyes.

My cousin was sort of fast. I would say, pretty fast, always going for the girls. I didn't have any special status, but I know that he was also sweet on me. He knew how to talk to a girl. "Have you heard about the seven-minute kiss?"

"*Eres un mentiroso, un gran* 'flirt,'" I would say, knowing full well that he dated many, many girls, something he admitted freely. I liked him, and he was safe for me. We weren't doing any serious stuff. Spin the bottle with his pocket knife, *algo así*. I had someone with whom to experiment a little, in spite of my shyness about these things.

One evening in the summer, we were probably both a bit lonely. "Let's go to the Inmaculada for ice cream and later head out to one of the piers by Amador. Have you ever watched the sunrise from one of the piers?"

The Americans had disposed of some canal-building dirt and rock, connecting the small islands of Naos, Perico, and Flamenco to the mainland. The strip, two single roads with small embankments of grass on the edges. On this pencil-thin lane, the ocean held you on every side. The city of Panama looked back at you across the water. Stone and wood buildings three stories high in the old city. Canyons in their infancy growing baby teeth in the west.

My cousin drove past a big wooden house with a cantina below and continued to a small, secluded pier. He parked on the manicured grass. He took out a fishing line with a hook and put some bait on it, wriggly worms that I didn't want to touch. We sat quietly. This was unusual because my cousin loved to talk. A pink-

and-purple haze sprayed its pastel dust on the slight waves lapping on the pier. Then he said, "Let's forget that we are cousins, okay?" I had heard this before.

As it got black, and I didn't think we would make it until sunrise, the pace of kissing escalated and touching—mostly through our clothes. My cousin kissed me in a new way. It started as a normal kiss where our lips clamped like two fishes. Then his tongue was throbbing fast of its own accord, like a snake dancing on my tongue and reaching into my throat. It was intoxicating and I melted right into it. Nothing else existed but that tongue. My chest vibrated. I couldn't make it stop.

"I don't think I want to wait until sunrise." I said. My voice sounded hoarse. "I didn't tell mami I'd be out so late."

"*Uy,*" he flicked his wrist toward the water. "Your mother's fast asleep. She has air conditioning in her bedroom, no? She knows you are out with me." My cousin laughed a little but released me. He was good-natured, and he didn't want to cross any boundaries. And he had other game somewhere else.

We were primos after all.

"You don't need to come up," I told him. I had a key. It was tucked in my tiny purse next to the lipstick and eyebrow pencil. I slipped it gingerly into the key lock and twisted. As the door cracked, I saw mami almost directly across from me. She was lost in a trance in her blue translucent nightgown sitting by the telephone table looking away. I wasn't ready for this, still feeling confused.

She turned at some sound.

"*¡Marlena, he estado preocupadísima!* I've been so worried!" She pushed her thumb into her teeth and looked at me from a great distance. "*¿Por qué no me llamaste?*"

She started to sound frantic.

"Mami, Roberto! You are going to wake up Robertito!" I volleyed the shame to her. I couldn't have a conversation with her. No. No. Nada.

"Marlena, I was worried. Something could have happened."

"*Vete a dormir*, mami," I said sheepishly now, heading to the room that I shared with Roberto. "No one told you to wait and to worry. *¡No te preocupes por mí!*"

Mami looked beaten. She pushed herself up from the blond bentwood chair.

"I was worried, *mi hija*," she said softly, as she left for the bedroom in her pretty slippers.

¡No te preocupes por mí!

Mami Noticed

Mami noticed something.

"*¿Qué te pasa Marlena?* I see you *tan preocupada*."

"*Me siento mal*, I feel bad about . . . Margie."

"What's wrong with Margie?

"Nothing is wrong with Margie, mami! Margie is the sun with planets that make circles around her." I let out a squeak. I felt my face pull down and stretch out of shape, a hideous shape. "*¿Y yo, qué soy yo?*" I told her that I always compared myself to Margie.

Mami was surprisingly calm. She listened. After a while she said, "Let me make an appointment with Doctor Godoy."

"Who is Doctor Godoy?"

"*Mi psiquiatra.* Go see him with me, Marlena. I know he will help."

His face comes at me out of the shadows. The psychiatrist's face is a blur, dark hair probably. After one or two questions from him, maybe five, I blurted my terrible secret. "I am jealous of my cousin. *Celosa.*" I probably said this nasty word very softly—inaudibly. Then I said, "I love her so much," trying to right this sin. Margie and I were inseparable.

The doctor asked what I liked to do. I may have said I liked to draw, or I am going to college soon in the United States. Maybe, that I wanted to be an anthropologist. Or an art critic. Or something else. I know there wasn't much.

The doctor summed things up. "It's natural to compare yourself to a person you are very close to. Some day you are going to be doing something very special to you—when you are ready—and you will see more clearly who you are."

I folded this memory into some hidden part of me.

Mami's letter in May, 1963, after I returned to Massachusetts before the end of my senior year

> *Mi querida Marlena,*
>
> *Received your letter this morning. You really seem to be in a despondent mood. But dearest it's a stage of thinking you're going through. We all do this type of thinking once in a while, but it's strange with you that you should have it so young. I'll try to tell you what I know about life. Probably for the past months you've been having one disappointment after the other. What it is I don't know, but I know that there are a lot of disappointments in life. Life is not a bowl of cherries, but you're young. (I'm being frank, I'm not lying or giving you compliments, you might not even*

like what I say), good looking, intelligent, and a very cultured girl, but I feel that for <u>some reason you're not</u> making the most of these qualities. Why, I don't know. You're the one that knows. Look into yourself and find out what it is. People do like you and very much, but I have noticed that your character changes and you get moody and you <u>don't give of yourself</u> to other people. Try to do things with other people together, don't become dependent only on other people, but join and maybe you'll get such an enjoyment from these things that you'll find meaning to life. You're a woman, in college at Oxy, try your best to find some profession that you'll be interested in—also a man might come along that you might love and he will love you, but remember one thing—nothing falls in your lap. You have to go out for it. I'm not very good in expressing myself, but Marlena, give of yourself to other people. Take responsibility and do things.

Mami

A Daughter's Understanding

I'd saved mami's letters for years. I found them in a frayed cardboard box alongside yearbooks and other school memories, her handwriting angled and sloppy like my own. When I read the words today, I see mami's need to fill her motherly role. I imagine she feels grateful to know that she is needed. She has things to tell me. A life lived. She can see things I cannot see. I wish I'd been able to feel the love that I read between the lines.

Mental illness is a chameleon. Sometimes you see it, sometimes you don't.

FLYPAPER

Smog

When I arrived in the thick of September, an orange blanket hung heavily over the tiny town of Eagle Rock near Pasadena. The prickly haze made our eyes tear. It scratched at the top of our throats. "Go West, young man," I'd learned this in my studies in the Northeast. Who was I talking to so many times from the payphone in the lobby at Haines Hall, crossing the red desert of Arizona, the whole of Mexico and Central America until my voice reached my "s" shaped cocoon, "centro del mundo, corazón del universo?"

Memories drift, thin-walled bubbles that threaten to burst. I see Lillian's face with a bookshelf behind. A scrap of conversation survives.

I am looking through a diaphanous membrane at myself. A single contact lens sticks to the edge of the table next to the rumpled bed. I push up against him. The boy is humping. Skeletal panties try to resist the shy advance.

Sue, my first year roommate at Occidental, is gangly with Scotch-Irish freckles. We live in a girls' hall. That's expected. Curfew's at nine. Lillian, a junior from Shanghai, says men will go to other women even after they're married. "I'm okay with this," she exclaims. "It's good for the marriage." I'm holding my breath; Lillian is crazy. I'd sharpen my knives.

I push Sue to dress like a man, not hard, she's so narrow, and slick her hair back with spray. "Hide in Lillian's closet," I tell her. "Let's see what she'll do." Lillian is no mouse. She yanks our white cotton bras from the dresser drawers to conceive garlands in the lobby.

Sue laughs in high-pitched spurts.

She tells me I'm "buxom," that I jiggle when I laugh. I can pass for thin. The padding's in my middle and at the top of my thighs, then I taper out to thin. *Pero yo se.* I know. My shoulders, my arms, my narrow face: They lie.

I envy the all-American girl, athletic and long-legged. She belongs on this carefree campus on the arms of her college sweetheart. She lounges in the sun on the quad, the patio that joins the school buildings, exposed. With nothing to hide.

"Lofty"

The coin purse embossed with the head of an Indian is bursting open, but still I need more coins. "Hey Sue, can you lend me three quarters?" The operator will say, "What country do you need to call?" and she will interrupt me after two minutes to ask for more change. She knows the sound of each coin. To me the nickels, dimes, and quarters sound a little drunk as they flutter down behind the metal slots. I drop a few pieces on the floor, worried that she'll cut me off.

Professors from all fields convene at Thorne Hall to deliver

Western culture. Thorne Hall is set on tiered steps with marble columns and a pediment, Occidental's homage to the Greeks. "*Click*." Luminous frescoes by Fra Angelico are projected from slides on a portable screen in the dark. "*Click*." This is copious, extravagant bounty.

I gravitate to the Intros. It's good to start new. Intro to Psych. Intro to Anthro. The Old and the New Testament. Spanish Literature—my first reading of *Platero y Yo*, *La Celestina*, *Don Quijote de la Mancha*. I dream about Linguistics.

My eyes are fixed on him. He's milk white and disheveled. His two front teeth remind me of rabbits. Dr. Loftsgordon, our Intro to Philosophy professor, poses the question and grins: "What statement, if true, would cause you to change your belief?" The whole school is spellbound by "Lofty." "If there is no evidence you would accept that would disprove your statement, what you are saying has no value." He grins right on top of his bow tie. "Ho hum. It has no meaning." Lofty calls himself a logical positivist.

I remember the fringe of grass along the path. It was a cool night. I review the arguments for God, and know that I've known this for a while.

The "mystery meat" and a bowl of green Jell-O crash down on the floor of the Student Union. It feels like I've been shot. "President Kennedy's been shot," Susan tells me like a zombie. I've been in the art building all morning. Everyone walks as if in a trance. We don't talk. The TV in some building is the only sound. We gather at the screen for days, bewitched by the muffled drumbeat, submerged in our feeling. The white horse with no rider buckles. Jackie. Caroline. John-John.

I've been thinking about papi. It's been seven years since he died. In the morning when I step out of the shower, something thuds inside of me. It's loud. "God is dead." I weep.

Oxy is an island. The only way to get into Los Angeles is to have a boyfriend with a car. I've been crying again. Lillian says that I miss my family. She is a Psych major. She asks if I've thought of killing myself. I feel numb and uncertain and separate from the others. But Sue makes me giggle. I speak to the school counselor, who is very slight. He recommends a battery of tests to discover my aptitudes. When I come upon a question with a visual component, I fill with black pencil the circle of the non-obvious answer. So he says that I have no aptitude for art. Sue is as confused as I am. She meets with a science instructor to try to determine her major. "Maybe I should be a marine biologist." The teacher sweeps his eyes over Sue who's holding her elbows together as she always does. "But you look like an art major," he bursts out.

Sue looks up in December pleased at the overcast sky. "Christmas is near!" An overcast sky in the winter robs the orange lid of all color. In December we look up into nebulous murk.

In my psychology class, the book opens with new definitions for words that I already know. Why give all new meanings to ordinary words? I'm angry at the book. I walk on the edges of the school grounds where no one can see me. (I cut class, and I do it again.)

Almost everyone else has closed the blue-lined notebooks. I'm hunched over mine working the essays, trying to find the idea that will gather all the pieces together, an original solution to my dilemma.

Plainly I have no habits for persistence.

Or a specific goal.

Or maybe it is something else.

My sophomore roommate, Ellen, with light curly hair, is placid and pretty. Ellen is the only one who knows that I am crying every day.

The flypaper's there. It's hanging in the corner of a cozy room.

"¿Qué te pasa, Marlena?" Mami's on the other side of the pay phone.

"Nada."

It's easy to fly to it. It's a comforting place.

When I don't have you contrasting me, mami, what will I be? My eyes feel huge inside of my face.

Lifeline

Dear Marlena,

I am happy and flattered that you have had the confidence to tell me about yourself, tío Stanley wrote. Since your father died I have hoped to be able to fill that role for you, and now you have given me that opportunity. Both tía Connie and I love you as much as we do our children. So as part of this family I'll talk to you like I would to them and have done so as the occasion arose.

Very few of us between the ages of eighteen and twenty-four know what we really want to be and do, and have no long-range goals. And it is natural to be that way. How can we know when we haven't experienced enough?

You say that you have had no success in college and

that you are a failure to yourself and to us. Let me assure you that not one university student in ten has the insight into his own character you have into your own. If you have learned nothing else during the last year and a half, we are satisfied with your education to date. We are not in the least concerned with your worry that you are not getting enough out of college. Like all of us you will have ups and downs in one subject and another. We think your decision to switch your major to Art is very good and know that you will now have the motivation to concentrate on your subjects.

You also have to concentrate on something else, that for you is more important, getting your weight back to normal. You are never going to be happy with yourself while you are fat, so get to work on this right away. Though you have undoubtedly heard this before, I'm going to give you one more reason for doing it, and that is to prove your confidence in me and my confidence in you.

Don't go on one of those crash diets. Eat all the meat, fish, eggs and green vegetables that you want to. Lay off the candy, desserts, potatoes and fats of all kinds for the next year as of right now. Have tea, one slice of toast and a juice for breakfast.

After you win your private war against the weight problem you will have regained the confidence in yourself that you have lost. Never quit—in the language of the boxing ring, if you go down, go down fighting.

There is so much to say, you to me and me to you that we cannot say in an exchange of a couple of letters. Why don't you come down for the Xmas vacation and stay with

us at home? We'll tell Julita that we want you to stay with
Margie as you are losing touch with her, which is the truth.

In spite of tío Stanley's letter, I couldn't stop the downward spiral. I let my grades plummet. I left Occidental after my sophomore year.

We are handicapped. *Complejos* is the Spanish word—things that hold you back—hurts, wrongs and incapacities.

IN TRANSIT

Panchita

Panchita owned the place as much as anyone. She flapped her feet all over the apartment and into the little balcony. "*La con... sen... ti... da,*" Julieta said, stretching the syllables to give the word some ice. Panchita was enormous, it seemed to me. She was no more than a green, red Amazon parrot that walked on Johnny's shoulder, digging her gnarled feet on his back. The tip of her wing was clipped.

Johnny, my handsomest first cousin, was married to beautiful Julieta who had piercing black eyes and who was clever with words. Mis primos had invited me to stay with them in the third room of their apartment in Colón. (The second room was Panchita's.) In Panama's port city on the Caribbean, named after Cristobal Colón, other cousins had offered me a job that would help me get a work visa to the United States. I'd given up my student status when I decided to leave Occidental. I didn't fully understand what had happened to me at Oxy. I had stalled mid-stride, my front toes pointed toward the America of Alistair Cooke, my rear foot lingering on the America of Amerigo Vespucio.

Colón had sixteen streets crossed by avenues, a small grid.

Empty, compared to my city on the Pacific, the newer, white-stuc-co houses owned by *hombres de negocios* who managed the thriv-ing import and export businesses that brought buyers from South America and the world. Downtown on Front Street and Bolívar, very close to the ocean, colonial buildings with balconies on the second story had lively storefronts below selling exclusive goods from Europe. Lalique, Lladro, Capo di Monte. Tablecloths em-broidered in the Orient. Colón was Panama's second city on the ocean-to-ocean axis, a transit artery that had been the econom-ic heart of Panama for much of its history. On the small side streets—calle Ocho y calle Nueve—small grocers, *chinitos*, owned by Chinese families, sold mentholated Camel *cigarrillos*, two or three singles wrapped in paper, five cents of rice, *queso en bloque* cut with a string.

"You are using all the hot water, *pelaa*." Johnny teased me. I knew it was a real complaint. I also knew it was a tease. I was comfortable in this slightly wacky household. Julieta lay in the middle of the big bed with their newborn, a thin scarf careless on her chest. I could smell my new *primita* and watch her fingers clasp into a fist.

"Bit by a tiger," tío Clifford said, activating with his eyebrows a scar on his forehead the size of an egg. Tío Cliff and my godmoth-er tía Inés also lived in Colón along with a handful of primos and tíos. On my lunch break from work, I would ride with tío Cliff over docile residential streets to eat *sanchocho* with my *madrina*. Their cook, Edna, made the light soup with chunks of *ñame, yuca, otoe* and a square of *carne*. A preamble to the special event over a demitasse of strong coffee: hearing my madrina laugh, peals of ringing bells, merry and contagious.

All I had to do was ask, "Tell me again, tía Inés, in how many ways are we related?"

Here's what she said every time: "Tío Cliff and your father are first cousins, their fathers Samuel and Joshua Maduro, brothers. I am first cousin to your mother. You know *that*. Because your Amamá is sister to Anita, my mother. *Now*, your grandfather on your *mother's* side—Jicky—and my father—Osmond—were first cousins. So your mother and I are second cousins too. A string of laughing bells. *Y también*, your mother and I are second cousins *again*, because your Amamá and my mother were first cousins to my father."

My eyes glaze over. My madrina does look *a lot* like me.

In my ancestral line—since Hanna Sasso married Joshua Piza in 1816 in Curacao, five generations before mine—thirty-two people had married first cousins. There were sixteen first-cousin marriages layered over one another like decoupage.

In Transit

On weekends I would ride the Panama Railroad from Colón to stay at mami's apartment in Panama City. Mami and I had arrived at a truce. She would talk, as was her nature. I would *sí sí sí* what I could no longer hear. Her anxieties now about me spiked up my own.

At Front Street for the mid-morning train, I'd wait at the platform next to a black man dressed neatly in a white, short-sleeved shirt and narrow tie, or it would be a grandmother with her granddaughter, clips holding the little girl's braids tight over her head, the girl's socks matching the color of her pretty dress. It would be hot. My clothes would stick to me uncomfortably. The backs of the double seats inside the train would be shifted forward or back so that members of a family could face one another, though I'd be riding alone looking past the open windows at swamps, tall grasses, and jungle—bamboo reeds sticking up in low-lying water—scenes that made me think of Vietnam, deep in my consciousness after a year of campus protests at Oxy.

The railroad had been completed in 1849 for the crossing of the isthmus during the California gold rush, long before the canal had been cut along the same path. American towns, Canal Zone towns, now surrounded Colón. The conductor would call: Mt. Hope! Coco Solo! Margarita! Fort Gulick! Gatún.

I would sit lulled by the musical English of the Caribbean panameños, gazing at the gorgeous tropics, feeling somewhat removed in a kind of soothing transition. Holding on, still, to what I knew and I loved.

The Atlantic here in Colón is not as wild as the Pacific Ocean one hour and forty-five minutes on the Transístmica. I am bathed in the tide. The tide rocks my heart. I can exist on the periphery to be swept by the tide and washed off and cleansed like a shell, the sharp edges softened.

Around our pebbles of white in the center field of my vision are people *color de miel*, a warm brown or light copper—sometimes whiter, sometimes darker. Panameños meld into one another, gradations of color from white to black. Facial features morphing, a continuum, nothing sharp.

Mis primas and tías are the mirrors of me. I accept this for a while. Their love is the mirror that I need to look into. Their love washes over me like the tides. I will look into another mirror another time to find what I must find. I will edge along the boundaries of this and that and find a little curl where I can be comfortable. Port cities are places of transit.

There's flypaper hanging in a corner of a cozy room waiting for me. I know it's there, ragged now. Not much gumminess left.

New York

Though the apartment was in the elegant neighborhood of Madison and 62nd street, it was damp and small and old. Patricia and I had the full bed with two feet of dirty carpet around and a mirror glued to the door. My sister's roommate slept on the juniper-green sofa in the living room next to a narrow window to the alley. She wrapped every morsel of food in plastic. She was tall and grey and taciturn and spoke in a measured way.

After leaving Oxy at the end of my sophomore year and my stay in Colón, I'd flown north to New York to squeeze in with Patricia who'd lived in the city for a short time, first moving in with a second cousin, now inheriting someone else's roommate. Patricia had not lasted long with mami after high school. "*Había also que no te dejaba florecer.*" Something, she said, just didn't let you flower. Patricia had moved for a while to Amamá's, then on to the home of mami's oldest brother. "*Me sentí una cenicienta*, not really belonging." I agreed with my sister. In spite of the loving care from our extended family, Patricia was unfinished, as I was. We were trying out a brand new life, not unlike that of other working girls in the city.

It was the late 1960s. We wore suit-like ensembles with short skirts and very short coats. The cold assaulted my legs up to my waist as I stood in banks of snow, waiting interminably for the Third Avenue bus to move me uptown after a day of work. We sat on the grass over checkered cloths, a stole on our backs against the night air, to hear free concerts in Central Park: Pete Seeger, Mongo Santamaria, The New York Philharmonic. Betty Friedan's *Feminine Mystique* had been published in 1963. The liberation of pantsuits followed in the early 1970s. I could take long strides as I rushed on the streets of Manhattan, not held back by the pull of pencil skirts. At night I didn't mind the freezing cold as I rode the Fifth Avenue bus downtown alone to the ice rink at Rockefeller Center to skate, freeing my arms and flying, working on my figure eights.

Patricia began to design children's clothes inspired by the Guna, an indigenous group that live on islands in the Caribbean coast of Panama, mixing riotous fabrics in pinafore shapes. She landed a small order with Bergdorf Goodman, learned to cut patterns, named her line "Pata Pata," printing rolls of fabric tape with the two words bold-faced in red. The path of her life was now established: creating a clothing line, later—in Panama—helping women in far-off provinces become self sufficient by tailoring their own handiwork for sale.

I had found an entry-level job in publishing, then another, where I performed genteel, low-paid work, naturally gravitating to books. Looping curvy lines of shorthand, typing (slowly), gaining a toehold with English as a Second Language skills. Moving on. Learning the trade. Assistant editor. Book editor. I would be in transition for years, still wearing an accent, pronouncing bridge as "breege," adding a fourth "o" to "portfolio," jumping into Spanish when I was angry or upset.

Patricia returned to Panama. Carlos lived and worked in Panama. Robertito lived with mami. Hidden from me then, I had made a choice.

Your Feet Know

Where you are born, your feet are in communion with the earth. It is an unpaved road with crushed stones, loose on the path, the lanes bordered with purple bougainvillea vines, their waxy thorns clinging to the brick.

Your feet know. No mother to pull at you or to send you fleeing. Inside shoes that pinch or that were left in the morning sun to kill the mildew. Like your body, they accept the heat. Your nose fancies the smell of gasoline spilling at the rear of pickup trucks that lift clouds of dust on the half-paved streets of the city, or the fishy smell of the ocean next to the avenue.

When you leave your tiny land, the pad and heel of your feet make light contact with the ground, the arch doesn't descend.

TOPEKA

Robertito

"*Mi hijo,*" mami had whispered hoarsely, trying to protect him from the anger and commotion. She'd had a scary fight with her boyfriend, an American from the Canal Zone (a married man).

Robertito knows what to do. He is four and very brave. He closes the door to mami's apartment. He climbs down the single flight of stairs then walks two blocks swinging his arms like a little man, keeping it together. At the corner there's a thick half wall made of stone that he knows. His fingers push inside of his palms. He knows to turn right. Then he passes the house with the white fence. Then he crosses the street into the green lawn and trees of the El Madurito.

"Robertito," Juanita greets him happily at the kitchen door. "*¿Qué te pasa muchacho? Tu abuela esta allí muchacho.*

Behind the swinging door he finds her, knitting booties on the couch. He kisses Amamá as he's been taught, and her blue eyes sit on him gently. "*¿Qué pasó, que pasó?*" she starts, the timbre of her voice climbing. Then of course she knows, and she doesn't insist. Amamá is practiced at picking up the pieces of Julita. She lays down the blue booties and the silver needles and pats the cushion next to hers. Robertito is practiced too. He sits and lays his head on Amamá's lap. Amamá strokes his back again and again.

In spite of steady doses of pills that mami pushes down inside spoons full of jelly, her anxieties persist. The stress always surfaces as panic about her body and disease.

"Connie," mami will call her cousin, "It is time for me to go to 'school' again."

Eleven years after papi died and six years after she divorced Bob, mami was interned at the Menninger Clinic in Topeka, Kansas. She stayed more than two years, with one brief return to visit Roberto.

Like a basket of reed in the river, the family carries the little boy to safe harbor. Robertito, seven, moved in with tía Connie and tío Stanley until mami returned when he was nine, about to be ten.

Letter from Topeka

The ink ribbon wound inside the manual typewriter chooses to be miserly or generous. There are filled "o's" and "d's" and "e's." The letter "h" sticks and holds back; it doesn't always deliver. When she tries a wrong thought or her finger doesn't agree, Julita presses the crosshatch key, backtracking over the interloper.

Mami's sadness, her unrelenting anxiety went on and on for years. Sisyphus and the rock, punished by the gods.

My deares t Walter,

    Just received your letter and was delighted with it.
I read it several times as wanted to take it in. As
you w ere pointing out very clearly my problems and wanted
to remember everything so I could apply it to myself. But
my mind is so dull that I forget everything and I am not
then able to wor k out my problems and conflicts. Beleive
me Walter that's why I havent been able to get well. It's
now fresh in my mind what you told me, but even now I'm
forgetting it. You say the Dr. says that I am very competitive and I'm trying to figure out in what way, but I
think I know what way, as I'm always comparing myself to
other people and feel very badly when I'm not able to do
what some one else is doing and it confuses me completely.
It confuses me so much that then I'm able to do nothing.
I'm hooking a rug and I go very slow so I'm the whole day
of# comparing myself to the fast way the others are doing
it and it makes me feel very badly as I feel that even in
simple things I'm defeated by someone else. What I'm
trying to say that I'm not able to do anything w ell now.
I'm like a vegetable now. And I feel this lack of invel-
vent in my brains. I miss it as I feel like blank. And
unfortunately Walter this is truth. If my brains were
a little more sharp I would get well quickly. What I'M
going to try to do is make the best of my situation.   I've
expressed this letter terribly, even in that I'm defeated
as I forget words etc. and the way I construct my sentences
is very bad. I want to tell you so many things, but dont
know how to express it.

    Patsy was here this weekend. I was very anxious
and tense, and the Dr.'s restrictions got me.   Went shopping
Saturday but couldnt even enjoy it as was looking at the
time all the time. So I couldnt leisurely look around and
enjoy the shopping. Had to buy everything in a hurry. You
would think that wheny my family came to see me he would
skip all that. I tell him that it's diffucult to shop in
a hurry and very tense, but he doesnt pay attention to me.

Mami's letter to her brother, Walter,
during her stay at the Menninger Clinic.

Mami writes to her brother Walter from the Menninger Clinic
in Topeka, Kansas. She is forty-seven, and her three older children
are grown. Eddie, my father, has been dead eleven years. Mami is
still responsible for Robertito, now living in Panama with family.

My dearest Walter,

Just received your letter and was delighted with it. I read it several times as I wanted to take it in. As you were pointing out very clearly my problems and wanted to remember everything so I could apply it to myself. But my mind is so dull that I forget everything and I am not then able to work out my problems and conflicts. Believe me Walter that's why I haven't been able to get well. It's now fresh in my mind what you told me, but even now I'm forgetting it. You say the Dr. says that I am very competitive and I'm trying to figure out in what way, but I think I know what way, as I'm always comparing myself to other people and feel very badly when I'm not able to do what someone else is doing and it confuses me completely. It confuses me so much that then I'm able to do nothing. I'm hooking a rug and I go very slow so I'm the whole day comparing myself to the fast way the others are doing it and it makes me feel very badly as I feel that even in simple things I'm defeated by someone else. What I'm trying to say is that I'm not able to do anything well now. I'm like a vegetable now. And I feel this lack of involvement in my brains. I miss it as I feel like blank. And unfortunately Walter this is truth. If my brains were a little more sharp, I would get well quickly. What I'm going to try to do is make the best of my situation. I've expressed this letter terribly, even in that I'm defeated as I forget words and the way I construct my sentences is very bad. I want to tell you so many things, but don't know how to express it.

If I was only well, I'd like to get a job selling at a store. Right now I would like to leave this place go to Panama

*and start a normal life being a mother to Roberto. But I
know that I need the inner satisfaction, as trying only to
get it from Roberto would be bad for him.*

*Have to stop now as have to go to an activity. My love
to Betty. Please write Walter as love hearing from you and
I'm going to get well with the help of God.*

All my love, Julita

Patterns

Snow was falling when I climbed into a taxi that February morning headed to the Menninger Clinic. The evening before I had
flown into Kansas City from New York and taken the van into
plain-looking Topeka. Patricia had written from Panama months
earlier on the crinkly blue *Par Avion* paper, "When I saw mami, I
found her improved."

As we approached the facility, I noticed that the grounds were
impeccably groomed. A clock tower rose above the brick-faced
building. I paid the driver of the cab and pulled on the heavy door,
crashing into a woman who looked like me: a little older than my
twenty-three years with wavy brown hair, a long face, and serious
eyes.

I know that mami welcomed me with a grand smile. I know
she must have cried. But I would not have cried. I would have held
in my feelings to not get swept into the vortex of her afflictions.

"He's upsetting rather than calming me," she started. "In the
fifteen minutes that I have with my doctor, he picks at me for
unimportant things. Like getting late to a class." Mami looked
doughy, and I felt a slight revulsion at her.

"I agreed that I was not going to ask any friend to go to the movies for two weeks. But when I asked someone a few days later, the doctor was angry with me."

"Why couldn't you ask a friend to go out?"

"Because I get upset when they turn me down. I don't like him," she pleaded. Then Mami stopped. She pressed the fingers of one hand into her palm, "I have to control myself." She did this once or twice, and this was new.

I met with Doctor N two times over the weekend. "It's hard to tell of Julita's progress," he said. "Your mother has to control her emotions in front of her son, needs to develop a pattern, a job, or a hobby to hold her steady day to day."

"What will happen when my grandmother . . . dies," I cried out.

"Julita will always need support. A psychiatrist, always."

In a dreary monotone Dr. N described a long series of incidents. "Julita was caught smoking in bed. She doesn't pay attention. She doesn't stick to a schedule. . . ." His face looked pinched.

Mami has always been this way. Some of these my own habits. Doctor N doesn't mention mami's feelings or discuss a plan of action. This is the way that he talks to her! Mami is anxious and narcissistic, but she is also smart and kind. Dr. N was not making allowances for my mother the way that our family did!

The Menningers, father and son, are said to have introduced psychiatry to the United States. They condemned the condition of asylum facilities in the mid 1900s, committed to providing treatment in a humane environment, insisting that people with chronic disorders could lead productive lives.

I don't believe that mami's doctor can act in a way best suited for mami, I wrote to tío Walter that night. *For her to come to grips*

with her problems, she must have better rapport. Mami is a wom-
an-child with many set, undisciplined habits that will never be
changed. She needs constant reassurance and some fatherly soft-
ness. I have heard that a problem of personalities is common be-
tween doctor and patient, and the only thing to do is change.

Had mami played me?

The tears had arrived, but the words held me.

Tío Walter and Amamá were worried about the costs. *I hope*
that mami decides to stay longer, I wrote. (Mami did remain at
Menninger for another year.)

Mami had lost the privileges to go shopping during my visit. "On the day my daughter comes, he's mean to me," she said,
but we did celebrate by going outside of grounds for lunch. Mami
brought along Marie, a laughing, fat lady with teased hair, not
the kind of friend I had expected. Not Gene Tierney today. Marie
was a kind woman who could wham-bam a good joke. We ate at a
local white-clothed restaurant and sat in the chairs that daughters
and mothers filled year after year during matching encounters.
Mami, gracious to the end, did not repeat her complaints in front
of Marie. We spoke about places we would travel to some day and
about pretty dresses.

(Did we have wine?) We began with a toast and recited the
well-worn refrain, "Salud... .... pesetas ... amor ... y tiempo para
gozarlos." "Health, money, and love, and time to enjoy them."

Marie insisted, "pesetas for me,"

"For me," mami claimed, "salud."

Of course, "*para mi*—I will take amor."

LOVE AND MARRIAGE

Tooting Horns

"Bring us your old crackers and cheese, Frank. And a whiskey sour for the lady." Donald's hands curved gently inward as he bantered with the proprietor of the Irish pub in Greenwich Village. Piano-player's hands, I thought. I pulled out my drawing notebook with the black corkscrew spine. My blind date's tapered fingers landed on the gouged, dark wood table. "The situation was confusing in Santiago," he said. "There was so much poverty. There were seven political parties and people could not agree on the shape of an egg."

Donald went on and on about Chile. His six months in Santiago had been important. I couldn't help staring at his mouth. His moving mouth. His voice was deep and melodious. His puffy lips not like my own, tapering bow. He was all head. His brain had to be huge! I looked into his green eyes as I sized him up with my amber pencil. Light brown curls. Ears close to his skull. Small nose. Handsome. More than that.

"I had never been abroad," he said. "At the stadium for a game of *fútbol* I saw that *chilenos* ate peanuts. Unshelled peanuts. Same as at Ebbets Field in Brooklyn. This shocked me."

He spoke about "*béisbol,*" "*los lanzadores*" that he saw in Panama where he stopped for two days on his open airline ticket
with Panagra upon his return from Chile to New York. Donald
made faces when he spoke in Spanish, lengthening syllables with
a mock José Jiménez accent. Made me laugh. He'd traveled on
his own in Chile. The Woodrow Wilson scholarship had put him
on the plane during his junior year at Princeton with a theme of
his own choosing: to study the effects of the Cuban revolution on
the political life in Chile. An impossible, huge topic. He'd met
Senador Allende, he said. He'd found a room at the university and
read newspapers every day. Almost no one with whom to speak
in English. They pointed at him and laughed at his trench coat.
"Gringo, we don't wear raincoats here. *Ja, ja, ja, ja.*"

I listened. I'd ask a question or two. He said that I was soft. He
said I was "eclectic." "It's my best compliment," he assured me.
"You don't fit any pattern. You have a million interests," although
I hadn't said much.

Here was a man who was open to experience. Crazy and
exciting.

"Fire!" We heard the cry behind us. A fire in the kitchen sent
the patrons scrambling outside of the pub onto the streets of the
Village. Donald grabbed his trench coat with multiple buttons
and belts and pushed me out gently, his fingers pressed softly on
my neck. Three enormous fire trucks arrived. They clumped at
the edges of the small establishment, flashing all their lights and
tooting, easing our first-date nerves.

With his near perfect memory and passion for history and poli-
tics, Donald cracked open a door into the wider world for me.

Are You the Crazy One?

Within sixteen months we would marry. Families would meet. Donald's parents and siblings would fly two thousand miles to Panama for the event. We would be concerned about our best man, Steve. Donald's childhood friend from Brooklyn had a thick, red beard, and the military government in Panama was harassing hippie types.

Tío Stanley wrote, *Have Donald's best man shave his beard very, very close. He should wear a jacket, shoes, and socks!*

Mami had not yet met my intended. She had heard that Donald's stepbrother Joe had been a patient at Menninger during her stay at the facility. On the night that Donald arrived, mami burst in on him at the toilet. "Are you the crazy one?" she asked brightly.

We Kissed Through the Veil

"You look like an Arab lady," he said, which made me forget the tulle on my face. We kissed through the veil.

Tío Stanley looked down from his slender towering. He had walked with me to Donald across the ceramic tile of the living room floor. The ceremony in Panama had been private and small. The maid brought a white terry towel wrapping the goblet. Donald winced when he stomped down with his foot.

Mami had made arrangements for the party at an open-air room next to the Panama Bay. The stars were bright. The white-clothed buffet tables were set with trays of shrimp surrounded by red-jelly flowers. Mami had on a bright green dress, and her lips were fiery red. There were bowls of *seviche,* roasted meats—sliced—and *pancitos,* and the tías had stirred *una sopa borracha,* a cake soaked in rum, brown sugar, and spices. Primos y tíos served themselves from the buffet; the men dressed in guayaberas, the white tunic shirts that every man wore on special nights. Guests sat at small, round tables then moved to another with their next portion talking with everyone during the night. This was how it was done.

Lucho's nephew put his fingers on the black organ keyboard, and the drummer started on the *tambor*. It was a sweet rendition of the slow moving *"Taboga,"* a song of nostalgia for our beloved island in the middle of the Bay. I was yearning for the dance. This, of course, was not the cue. "No first dance, none of that," Donald had insisted.

My new husband was wearing a grey suit and red tie almost matching the clothing of his two near-identical brothers. The three had fine, light brown hair curling this way and that. Without my glasses, I searched for the white gardenia. I danced with one or the other brother. My family couldn't tell them apart.

Donald and I at our wedding. Tía Connie and Tío Stanley,
my guardian angels, looking on.

Donald discovered an audience eager for novelty, a baby-faced boy from Brooklyn at the circular tables. In Spanish he challenged my tíos about the comfort they felt at the apparent calm after the toppling of an elected president by the Guardia Nacional two years earlier. "You are selling your souls," he warned. Donald railed against convention. He wanted the truth without a trace of sentimentality. (Of course, he was totally sentimental.) I wanted to know, too, and not cover up. But, please, Donald, not on my turf. *Nosotros nos sobamos,* all of us more important than one of us. Be soft. Say what they want you to say. My family is my heart.

Donald. Not tonight.

Mami had arranged a trip to Contadora, an undeveloped island where water and food had to be brought in from the mainland. This is the island where the Shah of Iran lived briefly during his exile in 1980, before leaving for Cairo where he was granted asylum.

In the clear water of the cove beach I saw a deep-gray ray glide near my legs, the huge mantle rolling with the sympathetic water.

The tender care that my family had extended to Donald's family during the long weekend had been impeccable. His relatives were enchanted with mine: multilingual, Spanish Jews to their own Hungarian and Russian origins. There was a correspondence between our families in spite of the distance of time and place in our stories. Both were modern Jews who resisted dogma and old-world traditions. Donald had been exposed to a Reform rabbi who discussed the political issues of the day and spiked his sermons with a call to action. Difference was not an obstacle but something to be cherished. Just exactly what I knew.

On a visit to Kol Shearith, our best man, Steve, lingered at the
tall, thin marble plaques that listed the names of the dead. "But,
it's the same last names," he laughed. "Alternating at regular intervals . . . *de Castro, Lindo, Motta, Maduro, Cardoze, Lindo, Maduro, Cardoze, Fidanque, Toledano, Cardoze, de Castro, Fidanque,
Toledano* . . . You are replenishing the gene pool, Marlena. Those
sticky genes will thin out."

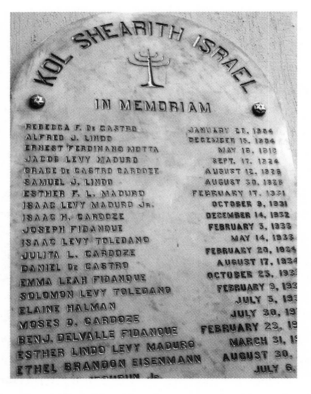

*One of several marble tablets that commemorate members of
Kol Shearith's community who died.*

It was time to depart, the moment in which Donald and I perform the romantic getaway pushed by handfuls of rice down the winding steps into the night. The rice was cast in our direction. My new husband picked up bits of the grain from the floor and flung them back. I turned, alone, looking at his laughing hair.

Sundays in New York

Sundays in New York my husband and I walked ten blocks along Columbus Avenue to a small storefront where I downed a white drink fortified with wheat germ. My body, I knew, was a temple for the life growing *en mis entrañas*. Everyone said, "This is a boy," but I feared a baby daughter. What kind of model would I be to a girl?

Our child was male, as foretold, our first born and the next. No fear of recognition. I could pour out my love, my held back love into these babies. I will not tear down. I will give. *El río se desborda*. I am overflowing.

Every year in the Northeast spring, I flew home with my American husband and babies. We stayed at mami's apartment. I nursed, and mami worried when the babies cried, "You don't have enough milk—they need formula." She gave lunches in our honor. Even then, if I held her apart, she couldn't touch me.

"I was walking on eggs," Donald says, "playing good husband material."

My brothers and sister took days off from work. My sister-in-law would drop todo and bring my two sugar-sweet nieces to welcome us. Almost everyone from this first *nido* would be at the airport upon our arrival, before taking us to my husband's favorite Cubano sandwich stop late in the night.

MAMI

Hermanito

The school bus leaves you on the side street because calle Cincuenta is crazy with traffic at four. I can see that you're beat after a full day of classes at Einstein. Even at four o'clock it's hot. You're pudgy at thirteen, Roberto, semi-blond like your daddy Bob who disappeared from your life. The same distinctive nose as his. But you are not tall.

The moment that you reach the apartment that you share with mami, you make a beeline for the kitchen, for the heavy *paila*, an iron pot, with leftover rice from lunch. You spoon a mountain of the soothing white onto a soup bowl—adding a chunk of butter. You carry it to mami's bedroom. For the rest of the afternoon—*gringuito*—it's American TV from SCN, the US military channel. Until mami comes home at six.

I see into her closet because the sliding door with wooden louvers has been left ajar. It's the wigs and false eyelashes time. I count five faceless foam heads with wigs.

At the makeup table next to the lime-green easy chair on which you have slumped, I poke through the drawers. I know that makeup table! It traveled from our house when mami sold it, long before you were born. The painted drawers are filled. Twenty small plastic boxes. *Germaine Montiel . . . Germaine Montiel . . .* I unsnap one of the clasps and touch the little hairy arcs. I wince. Enough. I've done my time, hermanito.

When mami's had her scotch and water, you sit down for dinner and return to the bedroom to catch the *novelas* with mami. *Simplemente María.* The one about the maid who falls in love with her boss and wins him in the end. On weekends I know you'll go with mami to her small cabana at the beach, and if she's short a fourth at bridge, you will be the fourth. When you are older you will drive her places. You will be organized. I understand.

Mami, with the doting help of family, is holding the fort. Leaving fathers—abandoning fathers—don't get blamed.

You are company for mami, hermanito, and she is your refuge, however impossible she is—or, can I say, monstrous? How are you coping, gringuito? I see something of me in you. The way that you line up your thoughts.

Merengón

In a black, dog-eared book that she kept by the phone, Julita inscribed her itinerary: Monday, groceries at Riba Smith; vegetables, el chino de Curundú. Tuesdays, lunch at home, bridge game, Club Unión. Wednesday, duplicate bridge. Hair salon, bank, lunch with Carlos, pay Enrique. On alternate weekends Julita left the city for her cabana at the beach, returning on Sunday at four.

When I visited from New York, I saw that mami was anxious still—and puffed greedily on her cigarettes—but seemed to manage within a carefully crafted system that she could control.

"Fill it, Gay, fill it to the top. Lois loves *guandú guisado.*" The deep silver spoons had to be overflowing when my cousin Gay served guests from mami's chafing dishes. She sat to mami's left. "My beloved Gay," mami would exclaim.

After her return from Topeka, mami hosted family and friends for lunch on Tuesdays, seating eight at the table in her modest apartment. Ivy, of course, was the cook, arriving every Tuesday— her stiff hair like a helmet—carrying a jar of home-made ginger tea in a paper sack and a special condiment for that day's meal. Ivy—born in Trinidad or Tobago—was short and stocky and lively. "Hola, Miss Julita!" she would greet mami as she wrapped her head in a triangle of fabric and started her work. She and mami were a practiced team, Ivy's specialties capped at the end of a leisurely repast with the habitual *merengón,* a layered ice cream cake with stiff peaks of meringue and amber chunks of caramel on top.

As soon as the confection appeared, like Alice in Wonderland's rabbit, mami would cry, "I'm late, I'm late. That horrible Ema will be nasty if I am late. Please stay and enjoy." And she would leave her guests for the bridge game that started at 2:30, Tuesdays, at the Club. There were moments that Gay noticed with alarm, when mami hung heavily over a corner of the table, elbows leaning into it for support, as she tried in this bent-over way to reach deeply into her lungs for air.

Mami also held lunches at the exclusive Club Unión where she could belong as *hija soltera,* single daughter of one of the founding members, my grandfather Jicky, without paying a fee, inviting Julia—her nanny companion late in her life—and Enrique, the chauffer, to sit and be served. There were brown serving brown, the bus boy and waiters calling her tía in deference while she called them *sobrinos*—my nephews—extending the compliment in an unheard of way that only she could pull off.

Julita surrounded herself with this other dependable retinue, the maids, hairdressers, and salesgirls who had limited options in a society built on privilege and class. She had the skill of decency—bred for generations—toward deeper-skinned women and men. She spoke in a proper voice and knew what was good service, seeing them more clearly—I conjecture—being herself a deposed queen but still bleeding blue. Obvious to all that she was a royal, one that they could laugh at or touch without fear of losing their heads.

"*¿Mi amor, cómo está el novio?*" she asked, cheerfully curious about a current boyfriend. At the beauty salon she maddened with her usual lateness but then charmed with her fawning, concerned about the health of the hairdresser's daughter with genuine feeling—certain that her own body was harboring the nasty disease. She bought foods that her maid enjoyed. If a *sirvienta* talked back in loose anger, mami might tolerate the affront, mindful that she herself was difficult. Or she would sit at the telephone table calling to find the woman other work.

Luisa

Mami's arms opened wide in a dramatic arc of welcome that was natural to her. "*Ay mi queridísima Luisa,*" she greeted the young woman at the door. Even though she had hired Luisa to paint her face, at four o'clock mami looked impeccable.

"*¿Cómo estás hoy, Julita?*"

"*Bien gracias, mi amor.*"

"*Bueno,* and where are we going tonight?"

"To a party at Connie's, Luisa. You know how I adore my cousin. I never see her. Her husband Stanley is to blame."

"*Pero* Julita, you know that if Connie listens to you all the time you are going to absorb her. *Tú bien que lo sabes.*"

"Sí, Luisa, that may be true. But I don't believe it."

Luisa is younger than me. She is light-skinned with a hint of bronze and smiling and likes to dress up. "*Con elegancia*," mami will say. A perfect woman for mami. Not anything like her daughters.

"Luisa, you are a little heavier there. Use a girdle, mi querida. A girdle makes the body used to being together. I am naked, Luisa, when I don't wear mine."

Two glasses of ice water sit on the corner of the dining table on a small silver tray. "Have some, Luisa." mami points to the water. "Let's go. I still have to get dressed."

The two move on to mami's bedroom, and mami sits down at her makeup table with a portable mirror in front. Luisa sits close up and assesses. First she will take off the existing makeup. They have their routine. Luisa is used to Julita who knows exactly what she wants, and besides, in Luisa's experience, she is one of the most *justa* persons *de clase alta* that she knows. She recognizes mami's fairness and honesty.

"I like to paint your eyes, Julita, they are really so expressive."

The *línea* was important. That's how they had met, at my uncles' store on Via España, where mami would visit every day so the girls would paint the black línea on the rim of her lids.

Amamá

"*Una vasta familia panameña está de duelo al haberse marchado para siempre Doña Esther (Essie) Cardoze de L. Maduro.*" The four-column obituary began with these words. I was in New York when I got the call. Amamá at ninety-two was dead.

We mourned her in New York, where a subdued group gathered tearfully for prayers. In Panama, among the mourners were thirty great-grandchildren, twenty-four grandchildren, seven children, the children and grandchildren of Amamá's sisters who had died years before, and all the other cousins of so many relations. Young and old with memories of Amamá at the El Madurito. Stopping at 1A for okra soup with fungi or tea in the middle of the afternoon. Amamá had not been the matriarch her own mother had been. Not the tremendous confidence. For Amamá, the elixir of choice was love.

Mami's an Orphan

"*¡Soy una huérfana!*" my mother, fifty-nine, announced when Amamá died. Patricia inherited the seven a.m. phone calls with the long list of recurring complaints: "*Amanecí mal . . . no puedo orinar . . . nadie me invitó,*" like a morning prayer, mami would begin. To Patricia the racket of the old matraca pounded at her ears. What to do but shut it down with a crash of the earpiece, knowing full well that another call would follow, until mami would tire and continue the prayer inside her head.

"*Luisa, mi queridísima Luisa.*"

"*¿Cómo estás Julita?*"

Ay, sabes, I have such sadness. I have been suffering so much since my mother died. My mother was the only one who loved me. I loved her so much. And, you know, I also loved my ex-husband Bob, but he did bad things to me. I am so alone. My daughter Patricia doesn't love me at all." Julita then aspirated on a long straw, her homeopathic technique for reducing her smoking habit. "*Es una terapia, Luisa.*"

"I understand it, Julita. Patricia probably has *un desamor*, a yearning for you that she cannot fill. You know that with your children *you* are the mother and *you* are the one who has to care for them." Luisa felt this truth deeply because she had been taken from her humble home of nine children and placed in her grandmother's care far from her mother and siblings.

The two went on to their routine. Sitting at the makeup table. Ending as always when mami would stand and lean toward the large mirror on the wall, look deeply into her eyes, roll back her shoulders, suck in her stomach, jiggle her shoulder pads in place, and look into her eyes again.

This Sunday mami would be taking Luisa and all her children to the Club Unión for lunch.

"You can save a few bucks this way. Order what you want," she'd add at the moment that she asked for two mimosas for herself from her sobrinos. She impressed on Luisa's daughter how to sit at the table.

"But, señora, why do I have to sit so *erguida*?" the young girl would say.

"Because you don't want to forget your elegance at the table."

Sometimes Luisa would drive mami to see people, sick people like mami's friend Carmen who was a "*viva*" according to mami. Or my great uncle, tío George, tía Connie's father. When she wasn't in town on a weekend, mami would ask Luisa, "Why don't you visit him on your own? Seeing you, a beautiful girl, he will feel better." (This was true.)

Over time, not having her mother brought mami a kind of release. Everyone noticed. While Amamá's apartment had been the midway of family life for decades, mami continued the luncheons that held primos together. She held the break fasts after Yom Kippur. Cousins got used to being family at tía Julita's apartment—tía Julita, a newly minted matriarch.

Though she had been dependent on Amamá for funds and at crises of one kind or another, mami now had a cushion of money in her own name, doled out carefully via interest every three months. At regular intervals she would be low in funds, *"Estoy mal de fondos,"* and would pester her brothers and later her sons to give her *"un adelanto."* She telephoned everyone until one caved in. Someone always caved in.

Tío George had a nickname for everyone. He got to calling me *"nunca cruces,"* "never cross," after he near killed me when I followed a ball in front of his moving car when I was eight. Mami he called "the brick."

Padrino

Mami begs for Essie, Carlos's youngest daughter. She spoils her with sweets and food and forbidden TV. When Emily the eldest agrees to join in, Mintz, as the granddaughters call her, takes them for long Sunday lunches at the Club. By mid-afternoon they leave for the new Yogen Fruz to argue the pounding heat with a frozen yogurt pureed with fruit to the texture of cellulose. To go, mami orders a pint with *maracuyá* and—Carlos driving—brings the girls to tío Walter's house. Mami summons the nurse and proudly presents the round, plastic container. "Quick, serve him quick! I brought his favorite. ¡Es maracuyá!"

"Essie, sing *'Cielito lindo'* for Walter," Mintz asks her every time. In the quiet of the afternoon, Essie's delicate voice climbs gingerly through the simple song as tío Walter sits on the reclining chair wrapped in a blanket savoring the yogurt treat.

The food that tío Walter eats passes through him quickly. His cancer is advanced. He eats mostly for taste as he has an ostomy. He is not squeamish and lifts his shirt to show his nieces the end of the intestine that is visible through the plastic bag. Mi tío is inquisitive as he always has been, weak as he is. The girls, who will both be doctors many years later, do not mind.

"With Julita," Carlos's American wife confesses, "I felt steam-rolled, ignored. Sometimes it's safer to withdraw. My excuse was that I had 'laundry.' I sent my children to their grandmother. Emily felt like Isaac, trussed up on the altar, waiting to be sacrificed. Essie was so petted and spoiled by Julita that it taught her grace—but it made her feel conflicted. I should have gone with them; children can't defend themselves. And yet, Julita was loved for who she was. She painted the world a different color."

A hybrid in my land of birth, my sister-in-law and I had switched places.

¡Esa Es Mi Abuela!

Dr. P had been making sounds filtered by his thick handlebar mustache. Emily couldn't read his lips, so she had given up listening. She was slouched back on the cushioned chair. Her long dark braid hung free behind the chair. Her boyfriend looked attentive. They were in a Medical Ethics class at the University of Panama. There were seventy students in the room curving alongside the tables arranged in a giant horseshoe around Dr. P. Everyone was dressed in white as was required.

"*Sí pueden.* You can indeed fire a patient you don't get along with. Take for example one of my oldest and dearest patients. I inherited her at Gorgas Military Hospital. She was a Panamanian woman from a good family who had privileges at Gorgas because she was married to an American at the time."

Emily wiggled her foot. "*What is he saying?*

"I returned to the hospital to make my rounds in the late morning, years ago, and witnessed an altercation, a woman making a scene because her doctor would not see her again. The receptionist grabbed me and threw the problem at me. *Me imploró,* 'Could you please take on this patient?'"

"*¡Esa es mi abuela!*" Emily whispered to her boyfriend, fully woken from her stupor. "It's my grandmother!" She clutched her overloaded fuchsia backpack.

When Emily approached Dr. P after class, he was in shock that inadvertently he had revealed the identity of a patient. But they sat and talked like colleagues. When Emily asked him for her grandmother's diagnosis, Dr. P said, "You know, in the thirty years that I treated her, I never figured it out." But Emily insisted, and Dr. P continued. "At times I thought that she fit in the category of *personalidad limitrofe.* At other times I would have said, *trastornos de ánimo.*" Emily knew the diagnostic terminology. Borderline Personality Disorder. Mood Disorder. Both pointed to a strong genetic link.

Emily had long made peace with her grandmother. "Mintz softened, as the years wore on. But when I was a little girl," she said, "I had absolutely no patience for my abuela and would deliberately do stuff that would drive her over the edge and stand my ground and never back down, throwing tantrums because I didn't want to go anywhere near her, and mamá and papá would make me. Mi abuela had no filter and said terrible things about my mother.

When I had to go, my mother dolled me up with bows and asked me to be sweet, 'Little girls don't tear places apart.' I would be sent to Mintz to hang around in the waiting room of beauty parlors or entertain myself while she made herself up. When I was older my mother explained that Mintz didn't mean to be the way she was."

YOUR SONG

Summer

Summer in Panama was the dry season—December through April—a subtle change from the daily rainfalls of July, August, and September, a gradual drying up of the skies, the air still humid but less so. The charge of green in winter that pushed against the roadways would ease, the sun bright as always, the beach the foreordained destination.

Married and living in New York, this is when Donald and I would visit Panama, then head to the beach with family. We would often land at mami's cabana, a square room with a double bed, a sofa and an L-shaped counter—the landing pad for bathing suits, cameras, and pre-made casseroles that mami brought to the countryside from the city. In this one year Donald and I had flown in with a plan.

Roberto was fourteen and living with mami. The two of them alone, not as in my childhood, where mami's neediness could settle over any one of us three—Patricia, Carlos, or me—to give the others a break. We thought of Roberto, a captive to mami's anxieties and harangues, our little brother, for so many years abandoned by his father. Roberto needed a break. My siblings and I had spoken by phone between Panama and New York. Donald agreed. It would do Roberto good, bright as he was, to escape mami's clutches during the school year, putting into gear the family tradition of prep school as an escape. Roberto could leave for his sophomore year in high school as Patricia and I had done. It was left to me to raise the subject with mami. We knew she would resist.

On the first day of the weekend, I couldn't find a moment to talk to mami alone. We had walked the long beach to the barnacled pool of rocks, climbed over the outcropping, and swum in the warm, salty water. We sliced the enormous watermelon we'd bought at a small stand along the road. Lunch, a siesta, and the day was done.

On Sunday we gathered on the manicured lawn outside the folding doors of mami's cabana where life spilled out: lounge chairs, a small table or two, a glass of scotch, or gin and tonic. Mami was happy. She had her children around her—all four of us—a rare thing. There was a friend from the Canal Zone whom she often brought along for company.

I knew I had to try. I stole a look at Carlos and Patricia. I pressed on Donald's hand for courage. There was laughter, jokes about bridge partners. I jumped in with my truth. "Mami," I blurted, my throat feeling like sand, my armpits hot. "What do you think, mami? It may be time to send Roberto to prep school in the States. . . ." A word or two only.

Mami blanched. Then she turned sharply toward me. "I know what you are up to," she growled. "*You* and Donald. Horrible people!" Mami looked hard at me. "You want to take Roberto from me. He is the *only* one of you who has ever loved me." She roared like a mountain cat, clenched her fingers, red nails ready. "You've all been plotting against me."

The rest of the day is lost to me. I, who could survive mami, now felt the deathly blow. I held my face together in public and pushed back what was building up inside of me.

I had loved her with my little girl heart.

I cried for weeks. Donald was worried about me after that. This set him hard against mami.

I Hold My Breath

There he goes again. Donald's eyebrows gather at his midline and the grooves on the sides of his mouth pull the lips down into a grimace. Just the face is frightening because it announces what is coming. An ultimatum.

"Julita, I will not stay at your apartment again when I visit Panama!" His body is hard with tension, and I have to choose.

If I fight with Donald in front of others he will congeal. I resist alienating my husband. Afraid of insisting, "This is my mami!" He can't make the leap. He's not schooled in the ways of family.

I will choose sides. I will swallow the indignity that Donald has aimed at my mother. Mami backs away. She will accept. She will not challenge him either. We are more alike at this moment. There are ways to submerge the pain. And ways to ignore it.

I Am an Organism

I have narrow wrists and pointed shoulders and a long neck. My eyes are brown. Sometimes they are blue. I have white skin, an inclination to art, to music and emotion. I exhibit a sense of caution. Julita is a part of us: one of the digits, a part of the hand. Linked to the forearm and the muscles on the shoulders, to the body that is me. The finger does what it can. It is not like the other fingers, and this makes me take special care. I am family.

Let Me See Your Softness

She had a huge desire for life because—all of us—she pushed us to live, an impossible need for the spotlight for her chance to get at some music lost to me underneath the static.

Let me see your softness, mami. What is the underbelly of pain that links you closer to me that I can understand and love you for? I saw it once and of course many times when your pain and frenzy prevailed, but that once when you visited me in New York and I did the proper daughterly deed of driving you to the pharmacy down the street to buy a tulle-covered cap to protect your hair during sleep and the ridiculous list of one dollar things that you bought, and I made dinner for you, but there was the fire-wall I'd built, and my voice was cool and guarded, and there was that moment at night when you were sitting on the sofa-bed—still a sofa—with its green-and-yellow plaid and tiny orange squares and your painted face crunched into the familiar creases. Though there was a glass half filled with water and pills on the table, you didn't reach for it but cast out with one breath the damning words, "Why doesn't anyone love me?" You didn't look at me accusingly, but I felt accused. Somewhere, I don't know when, I had stopped loving you, or I'd hidden that love to keep it away from tender tissue.

I don't want to be maudlin. I remember when we shared happy moments like decorating the house for Christmas with silver balls and limes and red *papos* from our garden, like proper Jews, and the star on the Christmas tree, not an angel, and the generous presents you insisted on buying for mis primos, and the crushing defeat you felt when my husband threw you a zinger from his own discomfort with your pain, his own pain and mine, from his lack of recognition of you. I don't blame him, although I should.

He said to me you were a "suit" pretending to have a life, a twelve-year-old girl, never a conversation, never a "you are a wonderful husband to my daughter;" instead you talked about your girdle.

"She created a stage set," he said, "this is the character that I am playing."

That is your song. The song that drove us crazy because it played and didn't stop and left no room for our songs.

Songs that keep us safe from the monsters. Play, play the music. Don't stop. I don't want to know what's under the bed.

I can't get into your head, mami. I still can't touch something real—real blood—mami. Your endless conversation kept you from knowing. The talk kept the monsters away. Your story song kept you from knowing.

Doctor P

Mami's psychiatrist in Panama since her two-year stay at the Menninger Clinic confided that at his age, "I'm eighty-five you know, I've seen a lot. There are fashions in psychiatry, *lo más importante de la época*."

He didn't know me when I phoned him from New York. He remembered, of course, his patient Julita. "*Apañé a tu mami de rebote*," he told me. We spoke in Spanish. I had to dig out mine as cleanly as I could. It tickled Dr. P to remember the moment when a nurse begged him to take on a noisy patient. Tired of Julita's late arrivals and complaints, another psychiatrist at the hospital had refused to see her.

While I was eager to find details in my mother's medical history, I had been reluctant to make the call to Dr. P, fearful of hearing a diagnosis that would impoverish mami's story, one or two words that would define her life with a single marker. Nevertheless, I ventured, "What was wrong with her, Dr. P? "

The line to Panama was uncertain, and as soon as a few words left my lips, his would break up. It felt like Dr. P was speaking to himself, lost in an odd reverie. "Classifications of symptoms are different in each country. In Canada, for example, they give more weight to culture." Dr. P added, "*La psiquiatría es imprecisa.* Psychiatry is imprecise. *Soy un escéptico.*" This word took me aback. While I knew where he was going, I had to look this one up. It sounded like "ascetic" to me, but then of course it meant "skeptical." I decided, I like this man.

"Your mami was stubborn," Dr. P said with some sweetness, still seemingly worried about Julita. "Your mami wanted *cariño*, went out with men for tenderness. They took advantage of her. She complained about not having money and depending on her mother. Amamá, no? Or her brothers. I remember Freddy y Arturo. I think Mikey played golf? Tu mami *hablaba en Spanglish.*"

Dr. P didn't seem to have memories of me or my sister and brothers. I didn't dare ask. Mami, I think, was done with us then.

There was a lull, and I pushed in a question, "How often did my mother have electroshock treatments, do you know?"

"*¡Psiquiatría salvaje!*" Dr. P exclaimed, admitting that he'd seen effective use of electroshock treatment but that years ago in Panama they weren't set up right. "The doctor didn't stay with you to make sure things were done correctly. It was used all the time, especially en *el manicomio*." El manicomio, the loony bin, put images into my brain of crazy inmates tearing down the hallways screaming. Of nurses strapping them down on *camillas* and gleefully prodding their heads with metal forks, making the poor souls stiffen until the movie screen blacked out.

"Yes, Julita did have electroshock treatments. But not in my time. Your mami was not psychotic. I never could find a proper diagnosis in all the years. I treated her symptomatically, supporting her day to day. I played it by ear.

"At the Institute for Living—*eso era un hotel*—they claimed that she'd had *un brote psicótico*." (I translated this as "a psychotic episode.") "At Menninger they wrote 'narcissistic personality,' but then," he said, "it depends on how you define narcissistic personality." Dr. P used some terms that he implied were the more extreme version, and I didn't want to interrupt. "But yes, of course," said Dr. P, "if we define narcissism as 'self-centered,' of course Julita was self centered. She was childlike. *Era infantil*. I can talk to you because it's been so long. And it's ethical. And you are close family."

"I heard her using the name 'Thorazine' as long as I can remember," I said.

"No, I never gave her Thorazine. That's an anti-psychotic. I gave her anti-depressive and anti-anxiety pills. She was a depressive. I could try to check, but I think some years ago I burned my old files. I don't think I have them still."

Thorazine was the wonder drug of the age that had transformed the treatment of inmates at insane asylums since the 1950s. Mami had been given substantial doses in the 1960s and 1970s, and she continued taking it for years. The long-term side effects of Thorazine are powerful. Was it appropriate for my mother? Did it confuse things? Did it help?

The time was getting late, and Dr. P was being generous with me.

"I think near the end, your mami did improve. She did learn to manage in a more realistic way."

HELIUM

Past the Swing Door

Past the swing door into the night, I searched for the telling shapes—angular for Carlos, soft and tentative for Patricia—in the small crowd of greeters at the airport. The notorious heat enveloped me. This was my second trip from New York to visit mami *in extremis.* After decades of sucking in the poisonous ambrosia, two packs of cigarettes every day, the emphysema had escalated. Again, mami at seventy-one was in the hospital, unable to breathe on her own. My plain-talking sister-in-law had called me, "Time to come. It's bad."

At the hospital in the morning, I heard the lively voices first; they were coming from a sunlit room opposite the door with mami's number. My tíos were there in the small *sala.* Some had stopped by before the start of their workday. *Habían* primos whom I hadn't seen for years and a young generation that was multiplying exponentially. The family was there to visit with "tía Julita." More would arrive in the days that followed, weaving with their stories and smiles a gossamer cloth of protection.

I kissed every one and then knocked lightly on the door. I entered with apprehension. Mami had clear tubes twisting inside of her nostrils; she turned at the slight disturbance of me. There it was, the scandalous smile. In spite of the distraction in her eyes, good breeding had come to mami's rescue.

My mother stretched her lips in a wide smile that exposed her upper gums. *"¡Hola mi querida!"* she exclaimed in a weak voice. I could tell that she was searching for the understanding of who I was and trying bravely to be capable. The constant smoking had ruined her lungs, and the intermittent lack of oxygen had ruined her memory. Mami had been on Thorazine and other tranquilizers for decades, a lifetime of addiction that made me suspect other kinds of damage.

My brothers and sister had alternated the all-night vigils; it was my turn to contribute—the forsaking daughter who had flown the coop. I slept in the hospital room for two nights in a chair next to mami, trying to make amends with my discomfort, until her doctor told us that little more could be done unless we wanted to intubate her permanently.

"Let her be," he told my sister when she asked him, "Doctor, if it were your own sister, what would you do?"

Mami left the hospital for her apartment. I was to stay with her during daylight, sharing a room with Patricia. Here, Julia, *"la nana"* as we called her, an enterprising maid on whom mami had relied for years, took the reins. She washed mami daily and cut her fingernails and massaged her body. I talked to mami clumsily by the bed. I read to her psalms from the Union Prayer Book. She eyed me warily in a semi-stupor. The heavy clay of her skin did not acknowledge me. When she felt a pain or had a fright, she called, "Julia, Julia. . . ."

I was there at her apartment in the El Madurito for a week. I was there by her side when her breath rattled one last time, as she struggled to regain it. I called my brothers and sister at work. I called tía Connie, who arrived breathless. Tía Connie screamed at the doctor over the telephone. "Isn't there anything you can do?"

Her flesh is dense and still, like wax. She does not see me. She does not see me. I had not visited this wounded place in a very long time.

Helium

Like a balloon that kept expanding, leaving no space, that's what it was. The helium of her body, so unstopping. I was squeezed against the wall resisting the pressure of her fullness. Some form was emerging, a kind of resistance flattened in me, not much helium in me.

Was it right that she went away for long months and years, leaving space for us to find strange, made-up shapes, not fully ballooning?

I see in my sister and brothers peculiar shapes, like mine. There is a logic that I'm understanding. We were shaped by her and by others, and the missing parts, the negative cutouts, are her. I find her there. Her shape against ours. She's part of us in the missing.

Now and then I think that she's a piece of the inside shape that is me. She left me gifts that I have unearthed in her letters and her story. Pay attention to living. Don't hold yourself apart.

My mother is dancing. She is laughing and her red nails are flashing. She is light on her feet. I notice the thin gold bracelet on her naked ankle. She is happy to be in a man's arms. She is feeling the wind. The wind and her body are holding on. Mami has never felt so good. She knows people are looking. She is free. Her brain is lifted. She is free of herself. I long for her. I held her apart and she knew that I did. I had to do it.

Sister Skype

> Casualmente
> fuimos a un lovely restaurant
> dentro de todo
> I can't complain.
> Patricia's the creative one.

> She nods.
> things are changing now
> swipes at her nose
> swipes on her ear

> We are mirrors of us
> today
> We Skype.
> her skin has sagged
> like mine
> rivers on my face
> our once clear features
> blending

hair
skin
teeth
eyes
blending yellow

She worries more.
I know what I mean and say it.
Of course she does
but nods her head
hiding

The Year 5779

It's the year 5779, the Jewish New Year on Tuesday, September 11, 2018. I've perched the iPhone 6 on the window ledge of my kitchen in New York. Patricia has just called using FaceTime.

I see Carlos! His narrow face, skin burnished by the sun. There's Martha, Carlos's wife. My nieces Emily and Essie. Roberto. They are moving in and out of the frame, looking into Patricia's iPad, adjusting the flip top to get the best view.

My siblings live in Panama, as does most of my family. They have lunched together after a Rosh Hashanah service at our temple, Kol Shearith, now moved to a new neighborhood in the rapidly expanding city. The "Paris of Central America," Panama City today looks more like Miami with towers eighty stories high, inhabitants of assorted skin tones and places of origin, as in the old times when the land was a crossroads of trade along one of the shortest spans in the Americas, ocean to ocean.

We sit in our respective cities viewing our selves. My body is captured in the corner of the screen, looking minuscule to me, enormous to them. I am happy to sit with my family on this warm September day.

Mis hermanos know that I've been engaged in book creation and near the end of the journey. While they've painted scenes for me from their own, still-tender stories, I'm not sure I ever asked, "What was mami's impact on you?"

Someone cries out, "You know, in spite of our wonderful family, I always felt homeless."

"Sometimes an orphan."

The next generation looks on as the siblings nod in recognition.

"You know," Carlos jumps in, "I didn't get to know myself until much later in life. And my relationship with mami changed. I learned to see through her difficult mental states and to love her as she was."

"The worst," Patricia says, "was the matraca. . . ."

I complete her thought, ". . . hammering at you."

Roberto lightens the mood. He shoots one of mami's famous sayings, "*Tu nombre es lo que más importa en la vida.*" Your good name is the most important thing in life. He laughs a full-throated laugh that sounds eerily like mami's laugh.

"Absolute good manners!" Martha calls out.

"Never bounce a check."

"Always answer '*bien.*'"

Patricia looks into the camera, her hazel eyes searching for mine. "During your writing of the book, what did you discover, Marlena?"

Is there anything I can add?

"Most shocking were mami's letters," I cry out. "And my letter to her when papi died. It's clear I needed a mother and felt that she was mine. There's the letter she wrote when I was in high school. Mami saw the despair that was beginning to seize me, said loving things I didn't notice until I read the letter now as a grown woman. She was trying to rouse me to action."

"Did the book change you?" Patricia insists. We've gotten closer with the resurrection of memories in the years of book creation.

"I think I needed to conjure up mami. To understand her, to make peace."

Tired after six children, Amamá tried to cope with an anxious daughter, doting on her, placating her. Mami was hungry for life. Once you start peeling back, your own pain becomes easier to hold.

"Her story has not changed, but I have changed."

ACKNOWLEDGMENTS

Thank you, Jackie Goldstein, Rickey Marks, Nan Mutnick, Eileen Palma, Jessica Rao, and Ines Rodriguez for your loving support on the long road of book creation and your sterling advice. Ahmed Asif and Nancy Flanagan, thanks for your faith in the rhythm of my words. Sarah Goodyear, first creative writing teacher, thank you for your encouragement. Sally Koslow, you inspire me with your work ethic and enormous talent. Patricia Dunn and Jimin Han, impassioned and wise mentors at the Sarah Lawrence Writing Institute, a thousand thanks to you. Nancy Recant and Susan Kleinman, I am grateful for your thoughtful insights about the book. To everyone at She Writes Press, thank you for ushering this work into the world with utmost professionalism.

Patricia, Carlos, and Roberto, what can I say? You've walked this road with me with such generosity. Martha Mae, Emily and Essie, Bobby, you have my back (and I have yours). To my extended family—primas, primos, tías, and tíos—some of you have gifted me with important details in the story. Rita, Julieta, Gloria, Margie, Stanley, Sita, and my beloved tías, I am deeply grateful. David de Castro, you have been an artistic guide and soul mate.

Thank you for the inspired title for my blog: *Breathing in Spanish*. Marce, thank you for the details you remembered so well. Arthur and Eduardo—my sons—Kelly and Emily, full daughters to me, you are beloved. You've made me a grandmother, the happiest condition. To my partner in the grand adventure of living—Donald, brilliant and funny man—thank you for releasing me way too many times to write and avoid writing this work and others. Your advice is always clear-eyed. Your love sustains me.

ABOUT THE AUTHOR

© Cathy Pinsky

Marlena Maduro Baraf has moved between the worlds of writing and design for much of her adult life. Her essays and stories have appeared in *Lilith*, *Lumina*, *Sweet Literary*, and *HuffPost*, among other publications. She lives in New York with her husband Donald. Visit her at www.marlenamadurobaraf.com.

SELECTED TITLES FROM SHE WRITES PRESS

She Writes Press is an independent publishing company
founded to serve women writers everywhere.
Visit us at www.shewritespress.com.

The Coconut Latitudes: Secrets, Storms, and Survival in the Caribbean
by Rita Gardner. $16.95, 978-1-63152-901-6
A haunting, lyrical memoir about a dysfunctional family's experiences in a reality far from the envisioned Eden—and the terrible cost of keeping secrets.

The S Word by Paolina Milana. $16.95, 978-1-63152-927-6
An insider's account of growing up with a schizophrenic mother, and the disastrous toll the illness—and her Sicilian Catholic family's code of secrecy—takes upon her young life.

Home Free: Adventures of a Child of the Sixties by Rifka Kreiter
$16.95, 978-1631521768
A memoir of a young woman's passionate quest for liberation—one that leads her out of the darkness of a fraught childhood and through Manhattan nightclubs, broken love affairs, and virtually all the political and spiritual movements of the sixties

Veronica's Grave: A Daughter's Memoir by Barbara Bracht Donsky.
$16.95, 978-1-63152-074-7
A loss and coming-of-age story that follows young Barbara Bracht as she struggles to comprehend the sudden disappearance and death of her mother and cope with a blue-collar father intent upon erasing her mother's memory.

Fourteen: A Daughter's Memoir of Adventure, Sailing, and Survival by Leslie Johansen Nack. $16.95, 978-1-63152-941-2
A coming-of-age adventure story about a young girl who comes into her own power, fights back against abuse, becomes an accomplished sailor, and falls in love with the ocean and the natural world.